CRACKS
IN THE WALL

RONNIE STALLWORTH, SR.

Ronnie Stallworth, Sr. Publishing

www.cracksinthewall.net

ISBN: 978-1-7355567-0-3

Disclaimer: Some actual names have been altered to protect identities.

DEDICATION

*This book is written in loving memory of my dad,
John Stallworth, Sr. I thank God for giving me the perfect
example of what it means to be a great dad. I miss him every
day and pray that I will one day be with him again in Heaven.*

ACKNOWLEDGEMENTS

This book would not have been possible without God giving me a supportive family and friends to encourage me along the way. I want to start by thanking my two sons, Ronnie Jr. and Jonathan. You two have been my biggest encouragers. Not only have you cheered me on, but our Stallworth Family Nights helped build father-son memories that make up significant portions of the book. Without you, most of my adult memories would be a blur.

To my brothers Michael, James, and my late brother Gerald, and to my mom, Rosetta, thanks for constantly asking "When will the book be ready?" to make sure that I stayed the course.

To my cousin Trudy Bourgeois, thanks for sharing your advice and network to help with advanced editing.

To Jim and Ouida Garner, thank you for really cementing the Gem Seeker perspective by looking beyond my unpolished exterior and helping me realize my potential. You didn't care what I looked like on the outside, how unpolished I was, or how shabby I dressed. You trusted me enough to invite me into your home, feed me, take me to yard sales (or "junkin", as you called it), and eventually helped me build a professional career.

I owe an enormous debt of gratitude to Mr. Charles Koetting, another Gem Seeker and a generous donor to the University of South Alabama. Your contributions have helped dozens of students realize their dreams of becoming engineers.

To Laura McCord, your advanced editing was excellent to help bring out more of the finer points in the messaging. Thanks for challenging my perspectives to bring more clarity.

I also want to thank Casey Cummings, Allan Dalgleish, Thomas Eberly, Cassandra Kellum, Lakshmi Mokka, Lewis "LD" Smith, and John Thompson for consistently nudging me to keep making progress and not give up.

Last, but certainly not least, to KishaLynn Elliott, my primary coach and ass kicker, I can't put into words how much I appreciate you professionally and as a friend for helping me with the lion's share of *Cracks in the Wall*, including the final cover and publishing. I'm very grateful to my friend Linda Moore for introducing us! You are a remarkably talented coach, writer, and encourager. Thank you so much for making both the journey and destination of writing this book worthwhile.

Sincerely,

Ronnie "Ron" Stallworth, Sr.

TABLE OF CONTENTS

PROLOGUE: THERE ARE ALWAYS CRACKS IN THE WALL

In life, we all face certain barriers to success. These barriers are walls that stand between us and our next level of growth. My dad taught me that if I look hard enough, I will see that there are always cracks in the wall; these are the weak spots. The goal is to persist in finding those cracks in the wall and press our way through them. We can't accept the notion that a wall has no cracks. Nor can we make excuses or blame others for the walls. We must make every effort to breach them. I've carried this advice in my heart all my life. Throughout my journey, I've come to understand more about the walls that my dad talked about, and the people on both sides of them.

On one side of the wall there are Hidden Gems, individuals that have potential but are raw in their current form. They are often underprivileged and/or limited by their disadvantaged backgrounds. They face their own tough situations with tenacity and perseverance, but their efforts are often obscured by their circumstances, lack of exposure, or the preconceived bias associated with their image. To the untrained eye Hidden Gems might look worthless, but they have tremendous value that simply needs to be encouraged. That value will be revealed exponentially when those who are willing to suspend judgment expose these Hidden Gems to new knowledge and opportunities. Hidden Gems must recognize and embrace non-monetary support as their highest priority in order to establish a solid and sustainable foundation for success.

On the other side of the wall there are successful individuals that are blessed with the ability to dig deeper and seek out the potential that lies beyond the surface of these Hidden Gems' perceived lack of aptitude due in part to their impoverished circumstances. These successful individuals are Gem Seekers when they exercise their passion and invest their time, energy, and know-how in exposing the Hidden Gems. They polish the promising attributes of Hidden Gems to a shine that can help light the world. Gem Seekers can overcome their fear of creating an entitlement mentality by providing non-monetary guidance, mentoring, and support until a solid foundation for success has been established.

We've all encountered these walls at various points in our lives and know the walls are real. Some of us, people like me, have been on both sides of it. The wall stands tall and can appear overwhelming with oppressive forces. But thank goodness these walls are not insurmountable; there are always cracks in the wall, as my dad insisted without reservation. Through these cracks, Gem Seekers can connect with Hidden Gems to help expedite their growth and maturity by teaching them how to thrive.

I was a Hidden Gem raised by a Hidden Gem—a single dad who was 62 years old when I was born. My dad set an undeniable example of what a great dad, and a great person, looks like. I'm now a proud dad, granddad, and Gem Seeker. By first telling part of my dad's story, and then my own, I will show the impact of the series of Gem Seekers I encountered throughout my life. Thanks to them and to my dad's initial influence, I've experienced remarkable success by anyone's standards.

Academically, I progressed from a teenager that couldn't read full sentences before the eighth grade to earning a chemical engineering degree and, later, an MBA from one of the world's top business schools. Professionally, I evolved from working over 100 hours per week on four minimum wage jobs simultaneously to becoming a vice-president of a Fortune 100 company. Philanthropically, I went from receiving temporary food stamp assistance from the government to providing dozens of chemical engineering scholarships over the years through the Stallworth Chemical Engineering Scholarship Endowment, which was partially funded through the support of generous donors. Personally, I went from scavenging the highways for aluminum cans to earn income in high school, living in a house that had no electricity, water, or gas and ultimately becoming homeless and living in my car for most of my senior year in high school to traveling the globe and living or working in over 70 countries around the world. Any level of success is possible when Hidden Gems and Gem Seekers are connected and form a bond. #gemconnection

I have an affinity for volunteering, mentoring, and serving others, and I have extraordinary empathy for people who are growing up with limited resources. Although I feel a sense of accomplishment when I reflect on my life, it took me over 30 years to get to where I am today. With more strategic and purposeful connections with Gem Seekers, it could have taken 10-12 years. I want to expedite the learning and maturity process for Hidden Gems who are in situations similar to my impoverished environment.

It has become a passion and a necessity for me to share the lessons I've learned as well as the personal stories of how I achieved success despite facing extraordinary setbacks that included a broken family, poverty, and illiteracy. The purpose of this work is to give examples of how to connect Hidden Gems who need help with Gem Seekers who have the ability and desire to help them without creating an entitlement mentality. My goal for Hidden Gems is to build enough confidence to take more calculated risks. This will expose their passion to learn and innate abilities and present the opportunity for others to help them reach their fullest potential in life.

And for the Gem Seekers who are taking this journey, I share stories that will help them recognize Hidden Gems in their raw state. My goal is to motivate Gem Seekers to reach out in supportive, non-monetary ways to better understand the dynamics of helping Hidden Gems. It will require Gem Seekers to start small, put themselves in the shoes of those who are poor and disadvantaged, and take action to experience the positive impact firsthand. It's exhilarating to see the difference a simple relationship or word of advice can make.

There is no better time than today to make this happen. If we breach enough cracks in the wall together, perhaps one day we'll watch it fall.

TRIBUTE TO MY DAD

My story begins with a glance back at my dad, John Stallworth. He had an indelible impact on my life and my current ways of thinking. He possessed the ability to overcome immense struggles with unwavering positivity.

My dad was the most important and influential figure in my life growing up. Even though he died in 1983 when I was 16 years old, he is still the person I admire most on this earth. The lessons I learned in those short years with him were so influential that I still often ask myself, "How would my dad handle this situation?" I loved his approach to nearly everything.

I grew up in Mobile, Alabama, with my father and three older brothers—Michael, James, and Gerald. The five of us lived so far below the poverty line that being called "poor" would have been a compliment. But I thought my life was great, and that's what mattered most. My dad never let us miss a meal or go without clothes or a roof over our heads.

John Stallworth was a real father and a true man. These aren't superficial terms or clichés. Common stereotypes paint Black fathers as harmful, violent, absent, and neglectful. My dad was a positive, constructive, and consistent provider. I have gained a great appreciation for the sacrifices my dad endured and the hardships he overcame to make our lives enjoyable. With my dad's love, my brothers and I were richer than most people, although we didn't realize it. #strongdad

People used to say wherever you find Mr. John, you will find his boys. We had everything we needed and some of the things we wanted, which is the right balance for everyone. My dad's "can-do" attitude oozed from every pore of his body to such a degree that all types of people would find themselves in awe at his persona and his presence. His actions were my first-hand lessons on how to live my life. That said, my life is a projection of the impression he left on me and others around me.

John Stallworth, my dad, was born on April 15, 1905. As the older son of Lorenzo Stallworth and Betsy (Montgomery) Stallworth, he was proud to share in the upbringing of his younger brother, Gradie. During his early years in Monroe County, Alabama, racism ingrained itself in nearly every aspect of his life. There were many reminders of this constant oppression that gripped America at the time. Black people were required to say "yes sir" or "yes ma'am" to any white person over the age of 12 or they'd be whipped in public until they complied. If they still refused, they would be found hanging from a tree before the next morning. It was disconcerting, especially for my granddad, a very proud man who had been born a slave. He didn't take kindly to being downtrodden and living under an umbrella of hatred. He realized he wasn't polished enough to hide his distaste for the racial disparities that Blacks had to endure, so he purposely avoided white people to minimize the possibility of being triggered by white discrimination. He knew if he lost his temper, he would put his family at an even more significant disadvantage.

No-Tail Bear

Black people were often called "no-tail bears" in those days. It was one of many derogatory terms that racist whites used to flaunt their perceived superiority and to humiliate Black people. At the end of his second-grade year, my dad was walking home from school when he heard a white kid yell to his father, "Dad, Dad, there's a *no-tail bear*! Can I shoot him?"

The sense of urgency in the boy's voice startled my dad. In an instant, he began running for his life across an open field, hoping to reach a nearby wooded area.

"Hell yes! Shoot him before he gets away!" the kid's dad yelled.

My dad ran with abandon through the woods and dense brush. Bullets sang past his head as he ran, knocking bark off the trees around him. Dad evaded the shots and eventually reached his doorstep. Once he was inside the safety of his house and his adrenaline level dropped, he noticed puddles of blood forming around his feet on the floor.

"Mom! Dad! Help! I've been shot!" he shouted.

As my grandparents frantically searched his body for a gunshot wound, they realized he was actually bleeding from dozens of cuts on his arms and legs. Thorns from the heavy brush in the woods had shredded his clothes and cut deep gashes in his arms and legs. Granddad was furious! He grabbed his gun, intending to go to the woods and take care of the bigots that had done this. He was going to protect his son, even at the risk of being lynched. Granddad was known for being tough. Even some of the white people avoided him out of fear.

It took several hours of pleading from my grandmother, my dad, and my Uncle Gradie to convince Granddad to calm down. Once he did, he realized his plan to take vengeance would probably get them all killed. It was a tough pill to swallow, but he did his best to let it go. The incident was a sobering reminder of the reality of the dangers of living while Black in America. Granddad struggled to overcome his anger from the attempted shooting. Routine racial slurs and constant threats of being whipped, shot, or hung took a mighty toll on his human soul.

The incident changed the course of my dad's life forever. In the early 1900s, there was no chance of a fair sharecropping arrangement. Facing impoverished economic conditions, the family made the decision that my dad would drop out of school. You could blame poverty, but the real truth was that my dad was safer at home than he was at school. My dad was proud that he accomplished his promotion to the third grade. It was a significant milestone for him. Very few Black people had any formal education at that time; most were utterly illiterate. My dad lived the rest of his life with only a second-grade education. He never returned to school after the attempted shooting.

Difficult times continued. One day my dad was entering a general store with Granddad near their home in the small city of Peterman, Alabama. A white man walked up behind them. When Granddad didn't hold the door for him to enter, the white man approached and began screaming obscenities at them. Granddad, realizing he was vulnerable standing there in public with my dad, took the tongue lashing. The best he could do to diffuse the situation was to retreat. He slowly walked away from the belligerent white man with my dad in tow.

Later that same night, several white men came to the house on horses looking for Granddad. They were calling him out to punish him for what was deemed as publicly humiliating the white man through his disobedience at the general store. Granddad knew the men who were yelling for him to come out intended to whip or hang him, but he wasn't about to go down without a fight. The men circled the yard, high on their horses, drawing closer and yielding torches. They threatened to set the house on fire to force him out. Granddad grabbed his shotgun. Grandmother hid near the back door with my dad and uncle, ready to escape the burning house if needed. Then Granddad began shooting through the front window at anything that moved. Every shot rang out, accompanied by my Granddad roaring at the men.

"I've had enough of you white bastards! If you come on my property again, I'll kill all of you!"

The white men and their horses scattered like roaches in the daylight!

Granddad was wise enough to realize the men would soon come back, possibly more of them. He stayed up all night with his gun, diligently keeping guard over his family, his home, and his life. But all remained calm. The following day, they learned that word had spread about what my Granddad had done to protect his family. The news had reached a powerful white family who had significant influence within the community. They knew Granddad was a man of integrity. The family quickly spread word declaring that the incident at the general store was insignificant and the threats against my granddad's family were senseless acts of bigotry. Soon, other white citizens in the small Southern town banded together in solidarity to block further retaliation against Granddad and his family. This experience is how my dad learned the value of integrity. From that point, he devoted his life to doing the right thing. Even if it seemed no one noticed, integrity would eventually prevail. #integrityprevails, #dotherightthing

🔹 Cracks in The Wall 🔹

The privileged white family in this story capitalized on a crucial moment to help my Granddad because they recognized him as a Hidden Gem with integrity. They were willing to look beyond my family's race and class and overrule the bigoted norms of society. Their simple act of speaking up saved his life because it extended their power to my family and mobilized a showing of community support from an unexpected source—other white citizen in this small Southern town. **When allies stand up to protect the vulnerable, it weakens the walls that divide us.**

A few years later, Granddad said goodbye to Stallworth Quarters in Monroe County, Alabama. He was plagued with nightmares generated by stories of a local Black man who had been pulled behind a horse with a rope around his neck until he was too exhausted to keep up. The man was then dragged along the ground until only pieces of his neck and head were left attached to the rope. Faced with overwhelming uneasiness around town, Granddad moved the family 70 miles south to Mobile, Alabama.

That's where my dad and my Uncle Gradie grew up. As the years flew by, Granddad and Grandmother passed away, and my dad and Uncle Gradie became full-grown men. My dad was so proud of his younger brother and the positive influence he had on Gradie's upbringing. According to my dad, Gradie was a very smart kid who was obsessed with purchasing something new and immediately taking it apart. He had a fascination with disassembling and reassembling items, learning mechanics along the way. That affinity helped him get a premier job at Brookley Air Force Base (BAB) in Mobile. BAB was Mobile's largest employer at one point, but, according to published reports, President Lyndon B. Johnson closed it shortly after Alabamians voted for Barry Goldwater in the 1964 Presidential Election. When the base closed, Uncle Gradie relocated to Sacramento, California, where he lived until his death in 1998. #betterlife

Working Man

My dad's evolution into a humble, forgiving, and peaceful man was astonishing given his gruesome memories of the past. He regularly had nightmares of the brutality inflicted on Black people in the South. Images of white people whipping, hanging, and terrorizing Blacks were relentless, and the ever-present repression never allowed my dad to ease his fear of the ramifications of non-compliance to white people. Even with his anxiety, my dad firmly established himself as a dependable, hard worker in the Mobile area. He did not take handouts. His philosophy was, "Always earn your way. If there isn't a clear path, then make one." Laziness wasn't encoded into his DNA. Dad also realized that sometimes we can't help ourselves completely. While some people have it harder than others, I learned from him that we all go through rough spots from time to time and might need temporary assistance, such as welfare. Dad insisted that this assistance be temporary and never permanent. He saw permanent welfare as debilitating to the progress of Black and poor people. He did everything in his power to keep our family out of "the system." He also helped others avoid the cycle of perpetual welfare dependence by connecting them to jobs and paths to earning their way.

☀ **Words of Wisdom** ☀
"Always earn your way. If there isn't a
clear path, then make one."
–John Stallworth, Sr.

Dad worked several different jobs simultaneously. He was a chef, a farmer, and a construction worker, among other things. My dad's skills in construction eventually landed him a job moving houses for a company called Schroeder House Movers.

During the 1950s and 1960s, many houses were built on cinder blocks versus slabs of concrete. This style of construction enabled houses to be more easily moved from one location to another. The work involved detailed planning and required the operation of heavy-duty equipment. Although my dad had minimal formal education, he possessed the skills and intelligence to execute these complex relocations of fully constructed houses through city streets without wreaking havoc. Over the years, Dad moved dozens of houses, including the house owned by the mother of baseball legend Hank Aaron. Schroeder House Movers became the preferred house-moving company in the area, largely due to my dad's excellent work. #smartafterall

Dad was also an opportunist. After spending some time moving houses, he decided to hone his knowledge of construction and increase his ability to execute other projects. As his relationship with Schroeder deepened, my dad was permitted to collect excess lumber and other supplies left over from house-moving jobs. Dad started collecting the excess supplies and eventually built a house of his own. He was thrifty with his meager salary of $2 to $3 per week. Then, Fred Schroeder, the brother of my dad's boss, cleared a path for my dad to purchase several parcels of land in Mobile Terrace and Cadillac Park, subdivisions located on the west side of Mobile, Alabama. #goodintentions, #relationshipbuilding

Dad's first house was on First Street in Mobile Terrace. Most of the parcels of land in Mobile Terrace were, by design, only 25 feet wide. The parcels enabled the construction of "shotgun houses," one of the most prevalent types of single-family dwellings in predominantly Black communities. The name "shotgun house" is derived from its narrow structure, with rooms directly connected in a straight line. If you shoot a gun through the front door, the bullet will pass through the house and out the back door without hitting anything. While shotgun houses lacked space and many amenities, they did provide a viable option for many Black families to own a home. #homeownership

As Dad took root in Mobile Terrace, he soon drew the attention of several young ladies. One was named Roslin—my mom. At 15 years old, she was much younger than Dad. However, they set aside the age difference and developed a relationship. My mom moved in with my dad, and shortly after, my sister was born. Unfortunately, she was premature, and technology wasn't advanced enough to help her survive. She passed away only seven days after her birth. She was the only girl born into the family.

My mom had given birth to four boys before I was born in January of 1967. Even prior to my birth, the family had outgrown my dad's limited house-moving salary, so he expanded his farming business by working out an arrangement with a local and prominent landowner, Shine Turner. Dad's farming business grew quickly, and as it did, he needed more pesticides to protect his crops. He stored them in a shed behind the house in Mobile Terrace. That decision proved to be a turning point in my dad's life. Three years before I was born, one of my older brothers, John Jr., whose nickname was "Dune," came in contact with the pesticides. He became very sick and died at age 3. My dad was devastated by the death of his son. From that day forward, he vowed never to use pesticides on any of his crops again. #familytragedy, #deathnotinvain

The tragedy gave way to ingenuity. Dad had a way of turning every obstacle into an opportunity. His crops still needed protection from hungry critters. But instead of pesticides, he built enclosures around plots of his farm using excess screen left over from houses he had helped move. The screens completely covered the area and protected his crops from insects without the need for pesticides. His pesticide-free vegetables were lush and vibrant, with no defects or damage from insects. Over time he became well-known in the Mobile area as the leading farmer of pesticide-free vegetables. His produce became so popular that people began making special requests for it. My dad was an organic food pioneer well before the word "organic" became popular. #organicpioneer

By the time I was born, my dad was nearly 62, and my mom was still in her mid-20s. They had inherent challenges to overcome as they transitioned through phases of their lives at vastly different ages. Shortly after my third birthday, my dad and mom separated. Their priorities had changed drastically, and the distance between them was insurmountable. My mom had been seeing another man in our neighborhood and had fallen in love. She decided to leave my dad to be with him. Her decision had a significant impact on all our lives. She was still young and had her entire life ahead of her. My dad graciously stepped aside so she could follow the other man she loved. Raising four growing boys was tough on my dad. However, he gladly accepted full custody of all four of us and took on the challenge of raising us on his own. My dad did a magnificent job caring for us as a single father while still working full time. It was a monumental task, but my dad never wavered when it came to taking care of his boys.

Although their marriage had ended, my dad treated my mom and her new man with the utmost respect. Their split was unbelievably amicable. So much so that when my mother and her new man had issues at their house, my dad was the first person they called. We all knew the guy she was with couldn't do basic repairs or handyman work, so my dad willingly helped them make repairs. Sometimes they couldn't afford to pay him. He'd still find ways to get materials and do the repairs at no cost to them. It was the right thing to do and provided an important example for us. Regardless of how we feel wronged by someone or a situation, it doesn't give us the right to sacrifice our own values. We still have the ability to do what's right and uphold our integrity.

Watermelon Wham

To further augment his produce business, Dad took advantage of supply and demand for watermelons in the Mobile area by closely monitoring peak and off-season harvesting periods. By watching these trends, he recognized the lack of variety of certain types of watermelons and the scarcity starting in mid-August each year. Most watermelon farmers in the Mobile area grew the same type of watermelon, a Jubilee. He expanded the local market by bringing in different types of watermelons, including Charleston Grey, Congo, and Sugar Babies from other parts of the state. After doing research, calculating costs, and forecasting the number of sales, he saved money to take trips to Birmingham to purchase watermelons starting in mid-August when local farmers had depleted most of their fields in Mobile and Grand Bay. Birmingham was 260 miles north of Mobile. At the large Birmingham Farmer's Market, he negotiated with watermelon growers to purchase bulk quantities of 500 to 750 watermelons for roughly $0.25 to $0.35 each, knowing that he could bring them to Mobile and sell them for $1.00 to $1.25 each during the normal harvesting season. Toward the end of the season in Mobile, he could still purchase watermelons for the same low price in Birmingham and sell them for $1.50 to $1.75 each from mid-August to early October each year. For a person with very little formal education, he was a creative and savvy businessman. This supply and demand strategy worked well for my dad over the years. Soon my dad became popular for selling watermelons along with other vegetables in the Mobile area. #creativity, #risktaking

My brothers and I often joined Dad on his trips to Birmingham. Those trips were some of the best times of my life. My dad always made the experience interesting for us. Our old truck wasn't well-suited for high-speed driving on the interstates, so we'd take back roads where traffic was lighter, and speeds were relatively low. My brothers and I loved taking the longer scenic route. The road trips felt like great adventures and afforded us quality time to hear Dad's stories about his childhood. Sometimes we'd take the six-hour drive at night when it was peaceful on the roads with very little traffic. We'd arrive in Birmingham a little after midnight and park in the farmer's market parking lot until daylight. My dad let us sleep in the back of the truck where the watermelons would eventually get loaded. The nights were cool, and my brother James and I would lay on our blankets, claiming to see all kinds of strange things in the night sky. When the morning came, we'd all walk over to the Smokehouse Restaurant, next to the farmer's market, for breakfast. We didn't have a lot of money, but Dad splurged so we'd have a great experience.

After breakfast, it was time to work. My dad would quickly get a deal made, and we'd park our truck next to a truckload of watermelons that we just agreed to buy. The bigger guys would toss the watermelons over to Michael on our truck. I was small and skinny, so I'd help my dad stack melons or scurry to put straw between the layers to prevent bruising. The transfer would go quickly in the morning before the temperature got too hot. We'd be on the road back to Mobile by 10:00 AM. As my dad got older, he would let Michael do the driving. My dad trusted Michael and gave him a lot of responsibility, which he always cherished with great pride and diligence.

On one of our trips back to Mobile with a load of 750 watermelons, we made it from Birmingham to Thomasville, Alabama, which was one of my dad's regular stops to refill with gasoline. He knew if we were full in Birmingham with 20 gallons, we'd use about 15 gallons by the time we reached Thomasville, Alabama. Our truck was old, and the gas gauge didn't work. To check the level, my dad would stick a hose in the spout of the gasoline tank on the truck until it reached the bottom and then quickly pull it out to check the location of the wet area on the hose's dip stick. Over time, he had marked different levels on the hose to represent 1/8, 1/4, 1/2, and so on.

We filled up with gasoline in Thomasville, and it was a welcomed stop. There was barely enough room for all of us to fit in the cab of the truck. We had only one bench seat in the truck. Michael was driving, Gerald sat next to him, then James and my dad were seated on the right side of the bench seat. I usually sat on a small toolbox that my dad placed between his legs. It was just high enough for me to see over the dashboard. James and I were exhausted, and so was my dad. I begged him to let us ride in the back of the truck on top of the watermelons for the remainder of the trip home, or at least for a little while, until we needed to get more gasoline. He thought about it and decided that the three of us would find a comfortable spot on top of the watermelons and ride the remaining 100 miles of the trip home in the back of the truck. We took a few minutes to move some of the watermelons around to make a spot for James, my dad, and me. Once we got comfortable, my dad gave Michael the okay to get back on Highway 43 south for the remainder of the ride home. It was much more comfortable for all of us. Only Michael and Gerald were in the cab of the truck. James, my dad, and I were now lying comfortably in the back of the truck on the watermelons. We were partly covered with our blankets and laying on others, so the ride was peaceful enough for me to fall asleep shortly after we got back on the road. The next thing I remember was sliding down the highway on top of crushed watermelons and my dad yelling if I was okay.

We were involved in a deadly accident about 20 minutes after getting back on the road heading south on Highway 43. As we approached the intersection of Highway 84, there was no requirement for us to stop at the intersection. Our traffic light was flashing yellow, which meant traffic on Highway 84 had a red flashing traffic light and needed to stop. Unbeknownst to Michael, the car traveling westbound on Highway 84 did not stop as we reached the intersection simultaneously. There was a horrendous collision as the car hit the front driver's side of our truck. The car was speeding, and the impact overturned our truck with such force that it hurled the 750 watermelons down Highway 43, along with my dad, James, and me.

One of the passengers in the car was killed instantly. My brother Michael was pinned in the truck with a broken collar bone. The impact knocked Gerald out of the truck. He was somehow pinned on the ground, beneath the bed of the truck, with gasoline dripping on him from the spout of the gasoline tank. He had fallen into a ditch underneath the truck bed and fortunately wasn't crushed by the 2.5-ton weight of the truck. Incredibly, there was no explosion despite the fact that we had just filled up with gasoline 20 minutes earlier. My dad, James, and I were miraculously okay. The watermelons kept us from getting scraped and cut on the highway. My dad and I had only one minor scratch each, and James had a broken toe. It was truly a miracle after sliding more than 50 yards along the pavement on Highway 43.

These were not the only miracles at that moment. There was a hospital located at the same intersection of Highways 43 and 84. I ended up in the hospital parking lot. We were all fortunate to have immediate care as workers ran out of the hospital to help us on the scene.

Coming back to retrieve the wrecked truck a month later, we were able to survey the damage of the crash better. The impact had been so hard that it ripped the entire engine out of the truck and crushed the cab. More importantly, the small toolbox that I usually sat on was destroyed and fused into the mangled metal from the cab of the truck. There is no doubt that I would have been killed if we hadn't gotten in the back of the truck in Thomasville. Thank God for watching over us!

We survived the accident in Grove Hill, Alabama, but my dad's watermelon business did not. It was a catastrophic financial loss that devastated all of us. The accident ended our ability to transport watermelons back to the Mobile area. The truck had also been used for other hauling jobs to earn income. However, the biggest impact was to our overall mobility. That truck was our sole source of transportation. We never had any accident, health, or life insurance growing up. We were financially paralyzed because my dad had most of his money tied up in the supply of watermelons. They were all lost in the accident. It took over a year of sacrificing nearly everything for my dad to save enough money to buy another old truck that we could use for hauling. Even though we were in a dire financial state, my dad went out of his way to shield us from most of the sacrificing. The accident occurred in late August, and he still made sure we got small gifts and a new pair of shoes for Christmas like we always did. We also never missed a meal. At the time, I didn't understand the toll it took on my dad. After all the work he had done to build a little stability for us, he couldn't seem to catch a break. His stress level must have been through the roof, exacerbating his ulcers, but he didn't show it outwardly. #godsfavor, #parentalsacrifice, #nobreaks

All Poor People Aren't Poor

Most people in poor neighborhoods spend a lot of time thinking about money. They want to figure out how to get from poverty to wealth. Growing up, I didn't know what it meant to be rich. My baseline was formed by what we didn't have. By that measure, I was only able to conclude that we were poor.

In my naiveté, like most people, I viewed poverty and wealth exclusively in financial terms as a child. Being poor meant living in an impoverished neighborhood, getting government assistance, and barely scraping by on whatever living you were lucky enough to earn. Once I grew older and experienced living paycheck to paycheck at certain points in my life, I was able to reflect on all the misconceptions about rich and poor people that I had learned from my dad. Without a doubt we were poor financially. But my dad taught us that there was more to wealth than money. He constantly demonstrated ways in which common sense and wisdom were more useful than money. He instilled in us the value of non-financial traits, characteristics, and gifts.

※ **Words of Wisdom** ※
"There are a lot of financially rich people who don't know they are poor, and there are a lot of financially poor people who don't know they are rich."
-John Stallworth, Sr.

Dad would often talk about my great aunt, Mattie Allen. We called her "Bam-maw." Bam-maw was a humble woman who lived in the same poor neighborhood where we grew up in Mobile Terrace in Alabama. At the time, there was a constant flow of millionaire politicians in the state of Alabama and the city of Mobile going to prison for corruption and stealing. Dad talked about how these so-called rich people were some of the poorest people on earth.

Bam-maw, on the other hand, was born into slavery. She worked in cotton fields and did other menial jobs most of her life. She simply didn't have an opportunity to earn a decent wage during her working years. Because she was born a slave, it's hard to say what her exact age was. By the time I was born, she was already over 90 years old. According to a local newspaper article, she was the oldest person in the state at the time. I'd sometimes stop by her house after school. Bam-maw would be sitting on the screened-in porch, swatting at the flies that made their way through openings in the door. Although we had few direct conversations, I remember her as one of the most content people I knew.

Bam-maw didn't let the world dictate her happiness. She kept it simple and did whatever she wanted, ignoring the rules of behaviors considered taboo. People said sweets were bad for her. That didn't stop her from eating bags of peppermint candy. People warned that tobacco would kill her. That didn't stop her from dipping Bitter Garrett snuff from the time she was a teenager until the time she died. Bam-maw lived a joyful life by staying off the grid to avoid the judgment of others.

Money wasn't Bam-maw's primary motivator in life. I never knew her to mention it once. Like most people, I'm sure she would have appreciated having more than she had. But she didn't dwell on the things she lacked. She saw no reason to reach for lofty aspirations. Instead, she focused on the little things like cultivating her small garden and putting food on the table.

Bam-maw had a very long life; she eventually lived to be over 110 years old. My dad estimated that Bam-maw had handled less than $5,000 her entire life. Nevertheless, he considered her one of the richest people he knew. She didn't worry about gaining financial wealth. She found peace, comfort, and great mental wealth in living life on her terms. That brought her satisfaction and comfort until the end of her days. Dad made sure we followed Bam-maw's example of developing non-financial forms of wealth. However, he was careful not to condone the use of tobacco. #liveyourlife

Dearly Departed

By the time I reached age 12, my dad was legally blind. He couldn't do basic things around the house anymore. It was agonizing to watch as his condition deteriorated. I had always seen my dad as a man who could do everything. Suddenly he was in a state where he couldn't prepare his meals, clip his toenails, or cut his hair. We constantly went to the doctor, thinking he would regain his vision after a procedure. We would all be devastated when it didn't work. His blindness tested his resolve and his ability to continue to drive forward in life.

He also had stomach ulcers from taking care of us and dealing with the strain of my mother leaving. He could eat only baby food—anything else left him with terrible stomach pain. When I was 12 years old, one of his ulcers ruptured. He had surgery to remove a portion of his stomach. After the surgery, my dad began to lose weight rapidly. He struggled to maintain his weight, which was exceedingly difficult on his limited diet. At the prime of his life, my dad was a mighty 6 feet 4 inches tall and 205 lbs. At the end of his life, he barely weighed 160 lbs. We didn't have insurance and so we couldn't afford preventative care. He was wasting away into skin and bones and became frustrated that he couldn't help out as he was accustomed to doing. Witnessing his declining health took a huge toll on all of us as I went through middle school and into high school.

I felt the need to take care of my dad. Caring for him became more important than schoolwork. On the days I did attend school, getting back home to Dad was my top priority. I loved being around him, and he needed my help. Even though I was, at times, feeling helpless by his blindness, spending that time talking to my dad and hearing his stories taught me lessons to live by and created joyful memories I will always cherish. My dad had the heart of a giver, a deep sense of fairness, and a passion for doing things right. He taught us to treat everyone with the utmost respect and dignity.

My dad passed away at Springhill Memorial Hospital in Mobile during my sophomore year in high school. I was 16 years old. Though his body left this earth, taking any new lessons he wished to impart with it, he left his teachings behind in the way he raised my brothers and me. The lessons I learned from him are woven throughout this book the way they are stitched into the fabric of my character as a man. I feel called to pass on these lessons by sharing my story. I want to urge the Hidden Gems on the planet who are hiding their potential, or hiding from it, to come forth and learn what you need to grow. And for those Gem Seekers, I urge you to help make the cold, hard world a warmer, better place, just like my dad did. #bestdadever, #changingtheworld

MODEST AND HUMBLE
UPBRINGING

One Generation from Slavery

I learned about slavery in the fifth grade at E.R. Dickson Elementary School in Mobile. My teacher, Mrs. Velma, taught us that the Thirteenth Amendment had supposedly ended slavery in 1865, more than 110 years earlier. At the time, I didn't connect the dots, and the topic of slavery almost seemed irrelevant to me. From my perspective, slavery was a "single event" in time that had come and gone—a mere history lesson. In my profound ignorance, I concluded that once the last slave passed away, that ugly chapter in history was closed forever, and we should have all been able to move forward. With that mindset, I didn't digest the ongoing impact of slavery on me or have much of an interest in the topic as an elementary school student.

As the school year progressed, I recalled a few more classroom discussions about slavery. Even though I thought I had a solid understanding of the impact on past generations, I still didn't appreciate the ongoing impact on subsequent generations, including my own. In many ways, looking at the repressed condition of Black people, forced into poverty and endangered by racist violence, slavery still seemed to be happening. The periodic tidbits of history in schools only skimmed the surface about those who were directly impacted, and essentially nothing about their descendants. The reality is, even if the school had offered an entire class on the subject of slavery, at my stage of development at 12 years old, like most other kids my age, I still wouldn't have appreciated it enough to embrace the class. I didn't know what I didn't know. #majorignorance

It wasn't until midway through middle school that I started noticing some of the subtle remnants of slavery around me. I had noticed the slavery dynamic still alive years earlier with the way my dad interacted with the white man he worked for as a house mover. Slavery seemed like such a long time ago, yet many of the white people that Dad dealt with were still imposing a modified version of slavery. They controlled the lion's share of our income. Our future well-being was in their hands. My dad had limited options due to his lack of education, low-income, and caring for the family as an elderly single father. I imagine he had a perception that it was fruitless to challenge the status quo, especially given that he was nearing retirement age when I was born. Doing so would have generated considerable risk for our family and jeopardized his longevity with the company. Winning a conversation would have lost the war for him. Considering the risk, he begrudgingly stayed the course and accepted his current status at the time.

As more time passed, I realized many of my hang-ups, shortcomings, and limited perspectives about what I could potentially achieve in life were forced upon me. They were the result of what I had consciously and subconsciously inherited, and the beliefs permeated my mind through my dad's actions and my impoverished surroundings. My father was born in 1905. There were still emancipated slaves living at that time. Growing up in such close proximity to slavery inhibited my potential to gain knowledge and exposure to higher-level thinking during my formative years. Goal setting, financial literacy, and certain critical- and strategic-thinking skills could never be taught to us at home because my dad and granddad, descendants of newly emancipated slaves, had never learned them. The ignorance that was intentionally manufactured in Black people by the institution of slavery was an obstacle I had to first realize and then work to overcome.

🪨 Cracks in The Wall 🪨

Hidden Gems and Gem Seekers must realize and accept that there is a divide that intentionally separates us based on social constructs such as race and class. **Recognizing the obstacles that lay ahead is the first step toward overcoming them.**

I realized by middle school that our history lessons about the impact of slavery, racism, and racial disparities were one-sided and incomplete. Most of the focus was on the perpetrators. By doing so, it continued to give them recognition for their misdoings. There was very little content about the enslaved victims who overcame these barriers. They were denied opportunities to, among other things, become well-educated, break down barriers for others, and raise successful families, which would marginalize the very oppressors that diligently worked to impede their success. Our history lessons focused on the wrong people!

In 1981, the morning news delivered a profound wake-up call to me when a 19-year-old Black man named Michael Donald was abducted, taken to a remote area out of state, and brutally beaten. His abductors then cut his throat before bringing his lifeless body back to Mobile, where they hung him in a tree on Springhill Avenue. It seemed inconceivable that such a heinous crime could still happen, and less than ten miles from our house! I couldn't imagine what he must have gone through. Even though it was an obvious hate crime, it still took more than two years for authorities to investigate the brutal homicide actively. Black people had been emancipated from slavery more than 110 years earlier, but some people still viewed them as disposable as their enslaved ancestors were in America. Only after protests and demonstrations demanding justice did the FBI and local authorities investigate it for the hate crime that it was. Ultimately two Ku Klux Klansmen were convicted of the murder of Michael Donald. One murderer was sentenced to life in prison. He then appeared as the chief prosecution witness in the murder trial of the other KKK member involved in Donald's lynching.[1] The second murderer was sentenced to death and executed by electric chair on June 6, 1997. It was Alabama's first execution for a white-on-Black crime since 1913.[2]

The horrific murder of Michael Donald helped reveal to me how the hatred and debilitation of slavery were still alive and rampant in our country. The brazen brutality also unearthed the reality that slavery was not a one-time event in history, nor can the slave mentality be flipped on and off like a light switch. Slavery had nodes and tentacles, tangled and embedded into the fabric of American society in ways that would impact and inhibit future generations forever—including me. People like my granddad suffered directly, as slaves did, until their death. Not much was different during my dad's childhood. On paper, slavery was abolished with the Emancipation Proclamation of 1863, but Dad still dealt with every single aspect of it moving

---

1. http://bit.ly/michaeldonald (GRAPHIC CONTENT WARNING)
2. https://nyti.ms/2QDUuqZ

through life. The nightmares of violence, permanent thoughts of inferiority, lack of access to formal education, financial setbacks associated with sharecropping, land taken illegally, uncompensated labor that resulted in wealth for others, and many other forms of servitude fill the list of irreversible injustices. As Dad raised us, it became clear that my brothers and I were, in fact, only one generation removed from slavery. We were intimately impacted more than most Black people our age, primarily because our dad spent the early years of his life living under slave standards. #wakeupcall, #remnantsofslavery

In many ways, life resembles a relay race where each person on the relay team is responsible for running one stage, or leg, of the race. The performance of each person counts toward the overall team effort. No one person can win a relay race without it being a win for the entire team. Granddad Lorenzo and my dad ran multiple legs of the relay to put the entire Stallworth team in position for success, and that is absolutely astonishing considering all the obstacles they had to navigate. There is nothing about my successes, as one of multiple relay runners, that can't be credited to their extraordinary efforts. #relayrace

☀ Words of Wisdom ☀
"No one person can win a relay race without
it being a win for the entire team."
-John Stallworth, Sr.

With this realization, I became more interested in my dad's life. He often shared stories with us about what aided and inhibited him along the way. Remembering some of those conversations helped me gain a much greater appreciation for his common-sense approach. He remained humble and modest by focusing internally on what he had control over instead of allowing the prejudices around him to kill his ability to function on a daily basis. He was conservative in his aspirations, an influence of his lack of formal education. He preferred to focus on what he could do rather than overreaching and coming up empty. Fortunately, he successfully navigated monumental events that occurred in US history during his lifetime, including the aftermath of the separate but equal ruling (Plessy vs. Ferguson, 1896), World War I (1914-1918), the Great Depression (1929), World War II (1941-1945), and the Civil Rights movement, just to name a few.

Furthermore, my dad was able to gain resources and supplies from some of the same people who denied him income and respect. Like an alchemist who turns nothing into something, Dad used those resources to build the house that sheltered us. He planted a small farm that both fed us and earned money. From there, he expanded his business ventures into auto mechanics and hauling services. My dad was living proof that education is not a requirement to possess intelligence. Naturally, if my dad had been afforded a formal education and real opportunities had been placed within his grasp, as opposed to opportunity born from hardship, he could have seen extraordinary success in his life. However, the prejudices of his era forced him to drop out of school at a very young age, robbing him of his full potential. The institution of slavery was designed to keep Black people in this condition by creating an uneven playing field. Black people were slowed in the relay race just enough to give slave owners, sharecropping property owners, and their beneficiaries an unfair head start and advantage. #unfairadvantage, #levelplayingfield

💎 Gem Seeker Opportunity 💎

*There are plenty of opportunities for Hidden Gems to turn obstacles into opportunities, but most won't know how to connect the dots. They need a Gem Seeker to place them at a better vantage point and help them see beyond their circumstances. Most Hidden Gems living in survival mode are overlooked because of their struggle. **To spot a Hidden Gem, Gem Seekers must see what others don't see, and help those whom others won't help.***

In a similar way to my dad and granddad, my ability to realize what I was capable of achieving in life was limited by resources I couldn't access. Because I wasn't being exposed to other experiences, I felt limited. I didn't know I could be as successful as anyone else. I hustled in small niches instead of seeing the entire world as an opportunity. My inferiority complex and my naivete dictated a lower trajectory for my life. Hustling wasn't the only viable option for my brothers and me. But for my granddad and dad, in the absence of formal education, hustling was essentially the only viable route for them to navigate the challenges of their era.

Through all the misfortune and turmoil my dad endured, he relentlessly focused on molding our behaviors in a way that would garner respect. This was something he had control over as our dad. He knew that raising us to treat people with respect would provide more opportunities to expand our perspectives over time. Exposure to better ways of thinking was imperative for helping me abandon the slave mentality while still maintaining a humble, modest, and service-minded approach to life. #bigpicturethinking, #exposureiskey

Embracing Humility

When you grow up in the kind of poverty I experienced, it's hard to imagine putting others' needs before your own. We were already struggling just to hold on to the few things we managed to accumulate. People who don't have much can develop a sense of selfishness if they don't embrace the value of humility. Even though we lacked many basic needs, my dad made an indelible impression on my life. Through his actions, I saw how even a poor man could thrive by focusing on others versus thinking only for himself.

As a vulnerable kid and teenager, I was bombarded with constant reminders of my inadequacy. I missed more than 100 class days during my elementary school years because I didn't want to be in an environment with other kids who I felt were better off than me. My brothers and I wore clothes that were obvious thrift store hand-me-downs. We didn't have great hygiene because we never had running water. We were only able to take baths once or twice a week. That process involved using a milk jug that we washed and filled with water from the neighbor's outdoor faucet. We didn't have an indoor bathroom. We used an outhouse, which was unusual for the 1970s and '80s. I wouldn't invite people to my house because we didn't have an indoor toilet. From an early age, kids at school teased me for having an older father and for being visibly poor. Their teasing put me into a shell of shyness and shame around our financial circumstances. I didn't feel I had a choice about being modest and humble. Our socioeconomic status was on constant display. We were on free lunch at school. Our classmates could see us using food stamps at the local convenience store and laughed at us about it. The kids at school would tease us about the government cheese that people like us stood in long lines to receive. They would joke that while the cheese was delicious, eating cheese toast, cheese grits, cheese rice, cheese sandwiches, cheese everything for weeks at a time created unprecedented episodes of constipation. It was easy for them to laugh at discomfort they couldn't feel. Meanwhile, the irregularity was keeping me humble. #inferioritycomplex, #feeldiscomforttoappreciate

Recognizing my personal characteristics early on, my dad went out of his way to not only help me cultivate the goodness that being modest and humble could bring but also help me recognize when people were taking advantage of me. It's a complex and somewhat unnatural way of thinking that by putting others ahead of myself, I was really the recipient of the blessing. He also helped me overcome the misconception that being modest and humble was synonymous with weakness. In fact, he showed me the opposite—to be humble shows strength, not weakness. It is a liberating and powerful way of life that allows me to govern most of my own happiness.

He was particular about enlightening me on key elements for success. Most were centered on treating everyone with the same level of respect. He was adamant that a ditch-digger, a derogatory title that was used to describe a person of lower status in the community, deserved the same level of respect as the President of the United States. In his eyes, a person was a person, and we all deserved respect equally. Ironically, my dad personally struggled to overcome the racism of his early years that branded him with feelings of inferiority around white people. Nevertheless, his message and actions toward others were clearly visible and reinforced his words that equal respect should be given, even when he couldn't personally reap the benefits of such a decent way of thinking. #actionspeakslouder, #humilityisstrength, #giverespectperiod

☀ **Words of Wisdom** ☀
"Having respect for others doesn't
require others to respect you."
-John Stallworth, Sr.

During some of our conversations, we talked about both of us having the mentality of a servant and the heart of a giving person. It's like a double-edged sword. It's indeed a blessing from God, but some people also see it as a weakness they can exploit. If left unmanaged, it could lead to my detriment. As a role model, my dad was well-respected and highly regarded as having a unique mix of gentleness and strength. However, he acknowledged the tendency of some people to mistake his kindness for weakness. He sometimes mentioned it as a hardship. Kind-hearted people always had to be aware of those who would take advantage of them. Although I lacked the command and presence that my dad possessed at the time, I was encouraged when other adults praised me for being a lot like my dad. He showed by his actions that we can be modest, humble, and strong, all at the same time.

My dad's determination to stay focused on humility was contagious for me. Our mannerisms were similar, and he was a perfect living example for me to emulate. Even as young as eight years old, I realized my mindset was different from a lot of other people's. I willingly worked at the local Twin M Farms picking peas, beans, and cucumbers. During the harvesting season, I worked every Saturday, starting at 5:00 AM. Some of the workers saw it as a poor man's job that they were forced to do. They complained most of the day and begrudgingly did the work. As expected, they did a poor job and tried to beat the system at every turn. We were paid by the pound of peas and beans we picked.

Some of the workers would put stalks, under-aged peas and beans, and even rocks in their sacks to make them heavier. The owners, Henry and Wade Mitchell, wouldn't always check the contents at weigh-in time. As the sacks got consolidated in the trucks for local grocery stores, the identity of the perpetrators' sacks was lost. Unfortunately for the Mitchell's, the irregularities wouldn't be discovered until the grocery store workers sorted through the sacks. I felt terrible seeing people cheating the system and, in the process, harming the very people that were giving us a job. Even at eight years old, I knew without a doubt that the culprits violated the characteristic of humility.

I would never knowingly put anything other than full-grown peas and beans in my sacks, and the Mitchell brothers knew it. They also knew I was ready to work hard and earn my pay when I arrived, unlike some of the others that went out of their way to kill time. They secretly paid me a little extra for the good work I was doing. At the beginning of the day, one of the brothers would look over the group of 18 or 20 workers and say, "Stonewall!" He was notorious for forgetting or messing up names. He never called me Stallworth, but I knew he was talking to me.

"I need you to take six rows at a time today. The rest of you take four rows at a time, and whoever is putting rocks in the sacks, you're going to get fired if I catch you," he'd say.

A couple of the workers, usually the rock bandits, would laugh under their breath. Periodically, the Mitchell brothers checked sacks at the end-of-day weigh-ins, and someone would get caught with broken stalks and rocks in their sack. They'd get fired on the spot. But the Mitchell's knew all the workers were dirt poor, so they'd still pay them a small amount. It was another early lesson about earning my way and treating people with respect.

Growing up in my poor neighborhood, I saw other examples of behaviors that didn't always align with my dad's or my approach. Some families in our neighborhood had better paying jobs, nicer homes, and felt they were higher-class citizens. One of our neighbors had a different way of teaching his kids. He constantly reminded one of his sons, Mike, who was my age, not to leave the yard when he played outside. Mike's family treated us and the other neighborhood kids as if we were beneath them. Mike's father didn't want Mike playing with us. In his eyes, we would never amount to anything. He didn't want Mike tainted by association. Mike's mother usually stood in the doorway next to him, a silent symbol of solidarity with his condescending view of us. #rolemodelbehavior, #modesthumblestrong

🦋 Hidden Gem Moment 🦋

*When someone treats you as if you are inferior, let it be a motivating factor. Don't let it deflate you or keep you in hiding. Otherwise, you'll never recognize your own abilities enough to risk revealing them to the world. **Those who underestimate you can't see your potential. Shine your light anyway.** The Gem Seekers in the world will find you.*

Just as his dad instructed him, Mike believed and acted as if he was better than the rest of us. I remember how Mike would play alone in his yard with the store-bought toys he wasn't allowed to share. Meanwhile, like most poor kids, we had to be creative. Half of our fun was working together to come up with ideas for new ways to play. We played basketball using an old bicycle rim nailed to a pole on the edge of the street; we played innings of baseball using a broken broomstick and an old tennis ball. We had more fun playing with toys we invented from trash than Mike ever had while he played with his shiny, manufactured possessions by himself. Mike and his father's rejection actually motivated us to enjoy ourselves more, even though we were just poor neighborhood kids.

Mike's dad surely had good intentions for his children, even if he didn't share the same sentiment audibly or visibly toward the rest of us. The fact that they had a nicer house, drove a nice car, and wore new clothes made it seem credible that they were indeed better than us. After all, we were living in a shotgun house and couldn't afford new clothes. It was probably easy for Mike's dad to believe that Mike was going to make something of himself and that the rest of us had no chance. The reality is, Mike's dad was in a position to be a Gem Seeker by helping us learn a different way of life, but unfortunately the opportunity was missed. #missedopportunity, #motivatedbybelittling

💎 Gem Seeker Opportunity 💎

*Hidden Gems aren't polished. Gem Seekers must learn to look beyond the first impression of appearance. This is the only way to spot a Hidden Gem whose potential is greater than you can imagine. **Don't buy into what you see on the surface as a measure of value.** That way of thinking could set a Hidden Gem back more than whatever external circumstances they are facing.*

Poorly Educated

My struggles in school worsened between the ages of nine and 11 when the constant transitions of puberty descended on me. I was the youngest in the family. My dad was always cognizant of our age difference; it weighed heavily on him. His biological clock was winding down as he witnessed me growing up. He was elderly, blind, and suffering with stomach ulcers while I was getting acne and my voice was breaking. He worried that his days were short while I had a long life ahead of me. He wanted to see me mature to the point of self-sufficiency. He'd always say, "I just want the Lord to let me live long enough to see Ronnie be able to take care of himself." That was his prayer and mission statement that he used for my development, and he took it to heart. He spent more time with me, teaching me basic life skills to help me mature faster. He gave me more responsibilities. When we sold watermelons, he'd occasionally set up a watermelon station and let me manage all of it. I learned to deal with customers—handling money, giving change, and resolving complaints as I loaded hundreds of watermelons into customers' cars. I grew to be good at it. We're all good at something; we just need to hone in on it. #handsontraining, #accountability

☀ **Words of Wisdom** ☀
"Even people who aren't book-smart can have rich skills."
-John Stallworth, Sr.

My shyness, lack of confidence, and struggles in school were delicate focus areas for him. I didn't like school; my goal was to drop out when I turned 16 years old. Many kids saw 16 as being adult enough to quit school if they wanted to. I was so sure about quitting that I wrote it on the wall next to my bed, in crayon, when I was nine years old:

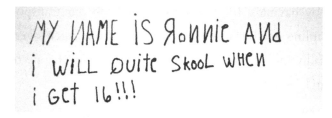

Dropping out of school conflicted with my dad's aspirations for me. He had to balance teaching me to manage my frustrations

with school with the equally important lessons that would help me quickly mature into a young man who could take care of myself. On the one hand, I needed to grow up fast, come out of my shell, and be more assertive in school and in life. But on the other hand, he didn't want to see me overcompensate and lose my humility. Ultimately, I couldn't bear to disappoint my dad or make him feel like he had failed to raise me right. By the time I turned 16, I had abandoned my foolish thoughts of dropping out of school. #highexpectations, #nodroppingout

The Shameful Chevy

In addition to normal challenges, there were also embarrassing situations that taught me valuable lessons in humility. A lot of my humility was tested throughout most of my elementary and middle school years while riding around in our sole mode of transportation, a huge yellow 1955 Chevrolet 6400 Series truck we owned. Since we were always in the market for work, we needed a truck that could haul large loads. We couldn't afford multiple vehicles, so my dad did the smart thing by having a big truck to cover both our transportation and hauling needs. He was very proud of our truck's versatility and gladly showed it off. On the contrary, I was happy to keep the truck hidden!

I will never forget one day he dropped me off at school in the truck. It was soon after the school buses had arrived, and my classmates were just entering the school. I begged him to drop me off at the corner of the street and let me walk the rest of the way, but that was crazy talk to him. My concerns about my classmates seeing me get dropped off in the truck were amplified when we got closer to campus and I realized the truck was too large to fit in a normal parking space. The only real option was to drop me off in front of the main doors of the school. Unfortunately, traffic in the drop-off lane was moving slowly. There was no chance of a quick drop-and-go situation.

The exhaust pipes and muffler system on the truck created a loud, raspy sound, and as we slowly pulled into the drop-off lane, the vibrations and roar of the engine attracted enough attention that most of the kids stopped and watched as we settled this huge two-ton yellow monster directly in front of the school's main entrance. I had no other choice but to get out and face my classmates. I quickly opened the door and, without making eye contact, tried to merge into the group of stunned elementary school students staring at me. In my haste to get out of the truck, I mistakenly left my metal Super Friends lunch box sitting on the front seat of the truck. I panicked, and before I could get back through the crowd to grab it, my dad laid on the horn to get my attention. Everyone jumped at the sound of the horn, which roared like a freight train. I was horrified as I climbed back into the truck to retrieve my lunch. My classmates later named the truck "The Yellow Monster" and re-told the story all year long, constantly gossiping about how poor we were.

I endured countless life events during elementary and middle school that generated gossip. My dad used to say, "If you don't have something good to say about someone, keep quiet." His only qualifying exception was, if someone is causing harm to us or others by their actions, we owe it to ourselves to step up and help rectify the situation in a positive and constructive manner. His advice suited me well because I had never been a gossiping person, and most of my friends didn't gossip to me because they knew I was not interested. Gossip simply doesn't suit me. When people have issues, they need understanding, not gossip. Unfortunately, when people gossiped about me, I didn't know how to handle it. Gossip is similar to someone walking around starting fires. By the time one fire is put out, there will be smoke in another area, and another fire to extinguish. I wasted valuable time trying to deal with gossip at school. Regardless of the good things others were saying, it bothered me when people gossiped about me, so I tried to extinguish it. What I didn't realize at the time was the drain that gossiping people had on my focus. It was giving them a certain level of control over my life. It was liberating when I accepted the fact that I couldn't control what others said about me. Although it was a learning process to remain in a good place mentally, the realization that people are going to do what they want allowed me to ignore most of the "useless chatter" almost overnight and remember another valuable tip my dad provided about people that gossip. He'd say, "Remember, Ronnie, that a dog that will bring a bone will also carry a bone."

If they gossip to you about someone else, they are certainly gossiping about you to others. Gossiping people are not credible, trustworthy, or genuine. When I started avoiding them like the plague, my life improved on multiple levels, including the volume of drama that I no longer had to deal with. I was free!

Dad also taught me to put the needs of others ahead of my own, even if others didn't realize or acknowledge it. He demonstrated this in simple acts like holding the door open for someone else. He would tell us, "Don't do it with the expectation of receiving gratitude. Do the right thing *only* because it's the right thing to do and for no other reason." Now, when people don't thank me, I won't be disappointed because I only did it because it was the right thing to do. If I do it for any other reason, such as receiving gratitude, I can expect to feel disappointment. Over the years, I've held many doors open for people who just scurry through without ever uttering a word of thanks, and I haven't been disappointed. My attitude is more important than their gratitude—simple but sage wisdom from a most humble source—my dad. #yellowmonster, #butterhead, #nogossiprule, #avoidgossip

☀ **Words of Wisdom** ☀
"Do the right thing only because it's the right thing to do and for no other reason."
-John Stallworth, Sr.

Five Elements of Humility

Modesty is having a moderate or humble estimate of one's merits and importance. Humility is being free from vanity, egotism, boastfulness, or great pretension and being courteous, respectful, and modest. These definitions describe how I've lived my life for as long as I can remember; even before I knew the meaning of the words *modest* and *humble*. When I think about their meaning more closely, it really boils down to five key elements for me:

1. Focus on the needs of others before your own.
2. Don't carry yourself as if you're better than anyone else.
3. Embrace the fact that there are many people who are smarter than you. Find them and learn from them.
4. Earn your way. Don't depend on or expect handouts. NOTHING in life is truly free, but God's grace.
5. Stay positive regardless of the situation. Positivity is always better than negativity. ALWAYS!

A DUMB TEN-YEAR-OLD ENGINEER

A simple definition of engineering is the use of science and math to design and make things. Engineers find solutions to problems, and that's what I did when I was ten years old. As early as the fifth grade, I had the desire and propensity to work on cars, to fix bikes, and to build things with my hands, even though I was unable to read very well. I preferred to remain at home tinkering with projects than to sit in school, trying to understand how the English lessons were relevant to my life at the time. I was also very shy and was too afraid to ask my teachers what they were talking about in class. This caused me to develop an alternative set of skills when I wanted to get something done. In school, math was boring. I didn't understand math in the theoretical way my teachers taught it. However, I innately understood the practical applications of math when I worked on my projects at home. I was able to use a feeler gauge to set the clearance on spark plugs and manually set the timing on car engines. I also figured out how to build a functioning birdhouse using a ruler, square, and angles. I would sell them to people in the neighborhood to earn money. At the time, I didn't realize I was using math or anything that was being taught in school. I only knew that while other kids my age were outside playing basketball, I was usually rebuilding a carburetor for a car engine.

I was content being virtually invisible in school to stay below the radar. My dad was 72 years old and wasn't in a position to monitor my school activities. In addition to not having the foundational knowledge to help me with my schoolwork, his vision was quickly deteriorating due to cataracts and glaucoma. Faced with his failing health, my dad gave me much more latitude to chart my own course than most kids my age.

At that time, my life consisted of missing as much school as possible so I could tinker with projects at home. I was absent from elementary school at least one day almost every week. There were always projects that needed to be done around the house. Occasionally I could convince Dad to let me skip school to work in the garden if a much-needed rain was in the forecast, to help him watermelons sales, or to chop wood for our wood-burning stove in the winter. Dad could relate to the manual work I was doing around the house. It was similar to his upbringing, so it wasn't very hard to make a case for staying home; it was real work in his eyes. He didn't keep count of the school days I missed, and I was particular to not miss consecutive days, which would draw attention to my absenteeism.

My oldest brother, Michael, was the right-hand man for my dad. He carefully watched my dad's every move and was always willing to take on additional responsibility. My dad trusted Michael as much as he trusted himself, and he could depend on Michael to deliver. Together, they could figure out ways to get almost anything done even if they didn't have the proper tools. Both were readily available resources to help me find solutions. Just like Michael, I was always willing to jump in and learn. #willingparticipant, #connectingthedots, #practicalapplication

Butt-Racer

Michael taught me how to build a butt-racer, a wooden car that we could sit in and ride down the steep hill near our house. There was no engine. However, coming off the hill would allow us to reach speeds of 15 to 20 miles per hour. The design was not sophisticated like a car for a soapbox derby. It could be made using old parts that we collected from odd jobs or items that were collected from the local dump. These parts included four wheels from a lawnmower, a couple of 2x4 and 2x8 pieces of wood, and a handful of large wood screws. After Michael taught me how to make the basic model, I immediately started thinking of ways to change the design to make it faster and improve the braking and steering. I also worked out the parts I'd need to add an engine so that it could go farther and faster than gravity would take it down the hill. I'd spend hours in my dad's shed, cutting and testing different lengths of wood, increasing and decreasing the wheelbase, and making other trial-and-error design tweaks. I didn't have a timer to compare the speeds. However, my brother's dog, Rex, would always watch me as I positioned the butt-racer at the top of the hill. Just as I started rolling, Rex would start barking frantically, chasing me down the hill. Once I got the design to the point that I could outrun Rex, I was satisfied with the speed of my butt-racer.

The next problem to solve was being able to stop. The original model didn't have brakes, and there was an intersection at the bottom of the hill. Cars didn't always stop at the intersection. Michael and his friends, who were older, didn't worry about the cars. They were crafty enough to avoid them. However, after I ran into the ditch a couple of times to avoid getting hit by a car, I decided to design a crude inverse brake system. I found a large spring in my dad's shed that was left over from one of his demolition jobs. I connected one end of the spring to a swivel handle next to the 2x8 that formed the center frame of the butt-racer. I connected the other end of the spring to a wooden paddle on the back wheel. Unlike regular car brakes, I had to pull the swivel handle back to release the brake.

In the process of testing the new brakes, I accidentally discovered a fun way to spin-out at the bottom of the hill. I tinkered with the butt-racer design for a few weeks to optimize it before I got bored with it and moved on to other projects. #problemsolver, #solutionfinder, #inquisitiveminds

An Engine that Could

Another one of my favorite pastimes at ten years old was mechanic work. It was a good source of extra income for the house, but, more than anything, I loved the fact that my dad trusted me to work on cars and trucks that people brought to him for repair. He trusted me to buy parts and install them properly. He would let me replace brake shoes, water pumps, starters, and other parts that wore out often on the older cars that people in the area drove. Sometimes he didn't even check my work.

Someone would occasionally need their engine rebuilt. My dad and older brother Michael figured out how to rebuild engines on our own truck and on numerous broken-down cars people in the neighborhood brought by the house. I intently watched every step, making detailed notes about the parts, order of operation, and necessary orientation of the parts. When the time came for me to rebuild an engine for one of Dad's customers on my own, I knew what replacement parts to order to complete the job even though I couldn't read a full sentence. With the customer's deposit, I would go to the parts store and purchase piston rings, inserts for the crankshaft, and all the required gaskets and lubricants. I would send the engine block to a machine shop to be machined. Once I got the machined engine block back and had all the parts, I was able to rebuild the engine and have the car ready for pick-up in less than a day. Learning these skills were not only helpful to me but were also helpful for Dad's mechanic business.

I actually learned to build a car before I even knew how to drive one. We had an old Chevrolet Biscayne parked in our backyard for several years. It was beat up, and my dad had no plans to use it for anything other than parts. After saving enough money from odd jobs, James and I purchased the required parts, made repairs, and were able to start the Biscayne's engine. My dad gave us permission to practice driving in the 40-acre field behind our property. We made a dirt track, ramps, and all kinds of obstacles in the field and used it to compare our driving skills. Gasoline was cheap, and we could drive all weekend for less than a dollar. We drove that old Biscayne for months until we finally broke the suspension trying to jump a 55-gallon drum. I learned to drive at ten and James at twelve in that junker we built. #daredevils, #driverseducationat10

Working with Wood

Next, I discovered a passion for woodworking projects. Two local cabinet-building companies had contracted with my dad to dispose of the mounds of sawdust and excess pieces of wood they couldn't use. One of those companies was high-volume and generated enough sawdust and scrap wood each month to fill a large bedroom in our house. My dad burned most of the material in a large pit in the back corner of our property. However, I'd always go with him to pick out pieces of wood that I could use later for building projects. He did the pick-ups twice a month from company locations, so I had a steady source of supplies.

These companies built customized wood cabinets, so the wood scraps had a wide variety of designs, and no two loads were the same. There would be a selection of multiple shapes and sizes of good quality wood for me to choose from for my projects. I learned the craft of woodworking from my dad, who had every woodworking tool imaginable, and from my oldest brother, Michael, who was also excellent with woodworking. He showed me how to make everything from rabbit traps to house shelves. Once he got me started, I continued learning by experimenting on my own, building birdhouses, gun racks, and squirrel and raccoon traps. I would use different saws in my dad's shed to make designs by trial and error. Some of my woodworking projects ended up in our firepit, but occasionally people in the neighborhood would purchase one of the projects. There was an old woman in the neighborhood named Mrs. Andrews who could cook anything—squirrels, raccoons, rabbits, an opossum sandwich—you name it! People would buy our traps, then trap animals to take to Mrs. Andrews' house to cook up and feed their families. It made me feel good to create something with my two young hands that met a community need and brought in extra cash for our family. #trashequalstreasures, #learnatrade

Booze Brothers

As our teenage years progressed, my brother James and I were determined to get more out of life. We spent countless hours thinking about how we could earn more money. We'd lay awake until late at night, trying to come up with new ideas. We were both feeling the pinch of poverty at school from not being able to purchase fundamental things such as a class yearbook or school pictures or basic football necessities. I will never forget the pain of being tackled and hit in the crown jewels because we couldn't afford an athletic cup to protect my private area. That happened so many times it is amazing that I was ever able to have kids! After it had happened a few times, Coach Brummer, my football coach at Hillsdale Middle School, bought me a cup out of his own pocket money.

By the time I reached the ninth grade, James and I were doing all kinds of odd jobs to earn cash—better known as "hustling." Hustling meant doing what you had to do to make money. Hustling wasn't an efficient or long-term way to earn money, but it was a viable option to earn small amounts of cash. Most of our hustles were time-consuming, difficult ways to make money. For example, instead of riding our bus to school, we would get up at 4:00 AM and walk the five-mile trek from

Mobile Terrace to Baker High School, picking up aluminum cans along both sides of Airport Boulevard. Selling aluminum to the local recycling company was a solid source of income. By the time we reached school, we were drenched in sweat. We smelled like old, stale beer from the cans that had dripped on our clothes as we carried the large, heavy sacks over our shoulders. We'd be exhausted before the school day even got started, which diminished our ability to learn. To protect our haul, we would stash the full sacks of aluminum cans in the bushes near the school until football practice was over. After a long day of school and practice, we still had to carry the heavy sacks of cans back home. It became increasingly difficult to wake up early enough to leave on time. If we didn't leave by 4:15 AM, we risked not beating the buses to school. We left late one morning, and the school bus that we normally rode passed us along the road. It was filled with kids from our neighborhood. James and I were moving as fast as we could to avoid being tardy for school. The kids laughed at us through the windows on the school bus as we frantically wrestled with the large, heavy sacks. After that, we abandoned our can-collecting venture on school days and only picked up cans along the road on weekends, school holidays, and during the summers.

Of all my brothers, James and I spent the most time with Dad during his last few years of life. James and I were still living in the same house and got to listen to Dad tell a lot of his stories. Many of them were enlightening, such as his perspective during the Great Depression. He intuitively thought the stock market crash wouldn't affect Black people because they didn't own stocks or businesses or have much of anything. But that wasn't the case. Black people were quickly pushed out of their menial jobs that others didn't want when times were good. Even farmers suffered because they were sharecroppers and didn't own the land. When things got tough, the landowners took more of the crops and profit or ended the sharecropping agreements altogether. Although it was illegal to do so at the time, my dad talked about making and selling moonshine to generate cash.

Since James and I were always looking for ways to generate extra cash, we listened intently as my dad gave detailed instructions about making moonshine. As soon as he finished with the story, James and I looked at each other with the same thought in mind—"Let's get into the moonshine business!" We started the day scavenging tubing, pots, and storage containers from Dad's shed to make our hooch. We mixed water and corn together in the container and left it to ferment. As the mixture fermented, it filled the air with a sickening stench as the alcohol built up pressure in the container.

The days passed quickly, and before we knew it the pressure in the mash container caused the lid to pop off. We knew at that point that the fermentation was indeed working. We decided to pull our first batch of hooch from the fermented mash directly after school the next day. We used the best strainer we could find to separate the liquid from the solids. The next step was to increase the alcohol content of the liquid by making a homemade distillation apparatus. We were afraid to use my dad's pressure cooker, so we used a can with a hole drilled through the lid to connect one end of the tubing to the container of liquid. We assembled the tubing and ran the coil through a container of cool water, watching it condense the vapors of alcohol. We watched our moonshine form, drip by drip, amazed by the simple operation.

Everything was going well except the speed. Not really understanding the process, James thought the five to ten drops per minute rate was too slow. From my perspective, it was a good pace to allow the steam to condense and also for us to make sense of what was occurring. However, James was impatient and insisted that I increase the flame on the stove. As I slowly increased the stove temperature, the drips increased to 20 drops per minute, then 30 drops per minute. James insisted that I continue increasing the fire. We got to almost a steady trickle, and we were successfully making moonshine. The dollar signs quickly started registering in our minds, and just as we started calculating how much money we could make in a week's time, the drips suddenly stopped. There was dead silence for about 15 seconds. We both quickly concluded that the tubing had plugged coming from our makeshift still. Before we could turn off the stove, there was a huge explosion that sent boiling liquid and fermented corn particles all over the ceiling, walls, floor, and us. It all happened so fast that we didn't have time to react. The popcorn-textured ceiling in our kitchen was ruined. The force of the explosion and heat from the still blew holes through the sheetrock on the ceiling and walls. Miraculously, we didn't get injured in the explosion. We successfully kept our elderly dad out of the kitchen for several days until the smell dissipated and the walls dried. The horrendous mess took us weeks to clean up. However, the impact of the explosion was permanent. There was still evidence of the damage for as long as the house was standing. #hustlingshortterm, #longtermstrategy, #overcomehumiliation, #enoughtobedangerous, #innovativesolutions

Blackberry Vino

Moonshine wasn't the only alcohol James and I learned to manufacture. My dad told us about making wine from blackberries. Our neighborhood had several houses that sold alcohol illegally. These houses were called "hit-houses." They sold shots of alcohol for $0.50 each, catering to people who couldn't afford to purchase a full bottle of alcohol. They also sold single cigarettes, knowing that many poor people couldn't afford to purchase an entire pack. Most of the patrons who frequented hit-houses were well-known. The biggest drinkers were known by their nicknames: "Big Eye," "Bootsy," and "Crocodile." They didn't have regular jobs, but they could afford to purchase single shots of alcohol. They were our target blackberry wine client base. James and I saw it as another opportunity to make extra cash. We could sell our blackberry wine for cheaper than the hit-houses. Without really knowing it at the time, we were exhibiting very good marketing skills by assessing our competition, performing segmentation to identify our target clients, and determining a competitive price-point for our product. The next step was to produce the wine at a reasonable cost.

We got thorough instructions from my dad on how to make our first batch of blackberry wine. We would take blackberries in a container and add sugar and yeast. If we added more yeast, it would ferment faster. Our goal was to get to market as quickly as possible. Adding too much sugar would ruin the taste of the wine, making it too sweet. Without enough sugar, the wine had a rotted, moldy taste that wasn't good. We had to hone in on the right amounts. Once fermented, instead of boiling it off like moonshine, we needed only to separate the berries from the juice using a strainer. We strained the mixture two or three times to remove all the pulp from the wine. If it wasn't sweet enough, we'd try to adjust it, but it didn't work to put in sugar at the end. You had to put in the right amount of sugar upfront.

After several iterations and lots of wasted berries, we settled on a mix of ingredients that made a decent-tasting blackberry wine. We bottled the finished wine in small re-used Coke bottles, the only thing we had at the time, and planned to sell them for $0.25 apiece. That was cheaper than the hit-houses, and we could still make a small profit. We tracked down Rich Jones, our first potential customer. The wine was similar to MD 20/20, a well-known cheap wine that we called "Mad Dog" because it made people act crazy after drinking it. Our wine was not as strong, but it was good wine. To our surprise, Rich Jones really liked it! Unfortunately, our patience was short, and with the fermenting time, the overall process was too slow for us. The $0.25 per bottle selling price for our product wasn't enough to keep us motivated. When blackberry season was over, we abandoned the venture after selling only a few batches.

With all my many ventures, from mechanics to woodworking to winemaking, I developed a variety of skills, including a knack for incubating ideas that I refined over time. Each one of the ventures was born out of curiosity to experiment and challenge myself to continue learning new things. Their success required planning, acquiring the needed resources, critical-thinking skills to connect the dots when I didn't have clear instructions, and a heightened level of passion and perseverance to execute the plans to fruition. Internally, I had the ability to accomplish great things but, at the time, I didn't recognize or appreciate my potential.

I was capable of learning and earning, even if my methods were unconventional. Schoolteachers teach kids how to approach issues and come up with solutions. Depending on their aptitude and interests, some of these students choose a path to engineering. However, I was terribly disconnected from my schoolwork while in class. I couldn't learn these skills in the traditional way. I spent my time coming up with alternative ways of addressing many of the same issues that engineers do, but without any formal training. In this way, I learned that there are many approaches to solving a problem. I had built an engine before I could drive, used common sense to make accurate measurements before I could read, and experimented with the composition of wine to refine the taste before I could legally drink alcohol. I was actually becoming an engineer at ten years old and didn't realize it.

We can't always judge kids solely by their grades in school. Anyone that looked at my grades at the time would have thought I had no chance to be successful in life. They would think I didn't have the intellectual capacity to learn or a passion for learning. Neither of these was true. I demonstrated my abilities in things I had interest in; many of them were engineering-related tasks I came up with on my own. I constantly expanded what I was capable of achieving through learning, exploration, and exposure to new ideas.

#knowyourcustomers, #marketsegmentation, #differentlearningstyle, #gradesarenteverything

🔹 Gem Seeker Opportunity 🔹
Schoolteachers are in a prime position to spot Hidden Gems. However, many are forced to deal with overcrowded classrooms. In a perfect world, teachers would have enough time to connect with each student, creating a customized learning plan. Less overcrowding would allow Gem Seeker teachers to identify and support students with different needs or tap into the potential of a shy student.
Better support for our teachers will lead to great things!

I DIDN'T KNOW WHAT
I DIDN'T KNOW

Education is learning what to know; experience is using what you know to discover what you don't know. Regardless of how intelligent we think we are, we've all had periods when we were naive, inept, were blinded by something, or have been sheltered to a point that we were unaware or out of touch with reality. It's important to realize that there is a spectrum of knowledge. On one end of the spectrum, we have ignorance, and on the other end we have mastery or expertise. The line that connects the two ends of the spectrum is the discovery of what we don't know. Ignorance isn't necessarily a bad thing. Ignorance, by definition, is simply a lack of knowledge, information, or understanding. I had plenty of ignorant moments where I made mistakes due to my lack of knowledge and exposure. But what I didn't know didn't kill me. My ignorance wasn't inherently detrimental, nor did it prevent me from learning or experiencing success later in life.

This understanding of the spectrum of knowledge gave me a new perspective going forward and helped me reset from my missteps. Ignorance is neither constant nor permanent. We can learn to move forward and improve. Growing up, I had ample opportunities to practice learning what I didn't know.

Hilben the Hustler

When I was 13 years old, my dad, my brother James, and I took a trip to a local grocery store. Hilben, a guy from the neighborhood, ran across the parking lot to greet us as we made our way back to our truck. He was well-known in the neighborhood for having a checkered history. He struggled with alcoholism and was in and out of jail for all kinds of criminal activity. The year before, he had been involved in an altercation with my brother Gerald. During the confrontation with Gerald, my brother James and I watched helplessly as Hilben pulled out a knife. Just as he did, my dad came out of my aunt's house to break up the fight before any physical contact was made.

On this day at the shopping center, Hilben seemed to be in his right mind and was extra friendly.

"Hey, can I get a ride back with y'all?" Hilben asked.

"No. I'm sorry, but I don't think so," my dad quickly replied, much to my surprise.

It was out of character for my dad to refuse to help people, even those who had a rough past like Hilben. My dad had a reputation for helping people who struggled to get jobs. Hilben seemed a little desperate and even promised to pay my dad if he'd let him ride on the back of our truck. My dad still politely declined. It was a sweltering day with the temperature above 100 degrees and near-100% humidity. Hilben was out of breath from the sprint over to us. Nevertheless, my dad didn't budge. I suspected it had to do with Hilben's history of criminal activity.

"I thought you were okay, Mr. John. Why won't you help me out?" Hilben questioned, still antsy and a bit agitated.

Even I was thrown off by my dad's resistance. My dad saw that Hilben wasn't going away. Maybe he also saw the look of shock on my face.

"Have you stolen something?" my dad asked.

"No sir, Mr. John! I'm clean. I don't do that anymore. I told you I'll pay you when we get there," Hilben quickly replied.

My dad would never charge anyone to help them. He always helped people for free. Not knowing his rationale for not wanting to help Hilben out with a ride, I was a bit disappointed.

After a bit more prodding from Hilben, while I looked on with dismay, my dad reluctantly agreed to give him a ride but only after Hilben let him check the contents of the bag he was carrying. James and I looked on intently, not knowing what he might pull out of the bag. Surprisingly, there was nothing in the bag but a shirt. James and I aimed smug, told-you-so looks at Dad as Hilben was deemed harmless. Dad agreed to let him ride on the back of our truck to our neighborhood. It was the first time I had felt a little disappointed in how my dad treated someone.

Hilben quickly jumped on the back of the truck and nestled himself in the corner, hiding from the bright sunlight. The rest of us got in the cab for the ride back home.

"Son," my dad told me, "I saw that disappointed look on your face. You can't always take people at their word. It could come back to bite you."

I told him I understood, but I really didn't. I thought he was being too hard on Hilben.

"Yes, sir," I said, and then I let it go.

We sat for a couple of minutes as if Dad were waiting for something. Hilben knocked on the back window.

"Mr. John, could we hurry up and leave? I need to get back to the Terrace."

The Terrace was Mobile Terrace, the neighborhood in the west part of Mobile where we all lived. My dad, suspicious of

Hilben's rush to leave, opened the door, climbed out, and walked to the back of the truck. James and I quickly hopped out as well.

"Get out of the truck," my dad told Hilben. James and I were shocked by my dad's behavior. It all seemed so odd.

"How do you plan on paying me when we get back to the Terrace, Hilben?" my dad asked. "You don't have a job. You're not earning any money." James and I were clueless as we watched the exchange.

Suddenly, Hilben reached inside of his pants and pulled out a pack of steaks, bacon, a bag of kidney beans, and a couple of onions from his underwear. We were all stunned! Unbeknownst to us, Hilben was running across the parking lot, and now hiding in the back of our truck, because he had stolen the items from the grocery store. He had lied to my dad multiple times about not stealing anything. Additionally, he was implicating us as accomplices, trying to trick Dad into being his getaway driver in our truck.

We knew my dad was pissed but he didn't show it. He was slow to respond but soon said in a calm voice, "Hilben, I'm disappointed in you. Not angry, but disappointed that you'd put my sons and me in danger with your lies and crimes."

His calm demeanor and pointed words seemed to resonate with Hilben, as they did with most people.

"Please forgive me, Mr. John. I'm sorry." Hilben begged.

"I'll forgive you," Dad said on the spot. "But don't ever ask me for anything again." Just as their conversation ended, police cars pulled into the parking lot and arrested Hilben for stealing. The scene was surreal as Hilben got into the police car.

"Get in the truck, boys," my dad said. We climbed into the truck, and we never spoke about the incident again. We didn't have to. #notguiltybyassociation, #jumpingtoconclusions, #trustyourgut

A Dirty Trick

I started developing an interest in girls around the age of 13. I wasn't even getting to first base like most teenagers were at the time. My eyes were open, but my mouth was sealed shut and I kept my hands to myself. My personality was cloaked in shyness that made it nearly impossible to talk to girls. It didn't help that I was also hearing horror stories from girls in my class about all the changes they were experiencing with their bodies during puberty. I learned that girls get boobs, pubes, and periods during that time. It was both frightening and intriguing.

My first kiss happened unexpectedly on a sunny afternoon on the north side of the bleachers in my high school gym. I was 14 years old. Her name was Trisha Johnson, and she was the same age as me. Even though Trisha was a very attractive cheerleader who was fully physically developed, hanging out with her was like hanging out with one of the guys. She was one of the most popular girls in school because of her strong, outgoing personality. She could have a conversation with anyone, even me, through my infinite shyness.

On this day, I was hanging out with Trisha and two of my friends, Chris Warren and Jeff Patterson. Trisha was getting up to leave when, without warning, she leaned over and smooched me on the cheek. It was over so quickly that it took me a few seconds to recognize that it had happened at all. I processed the kiss, feeling stunned, confused, and overjoyed all at the same time. I couldn't believe that she would kiss me so casually as if it was something we always did. I never had any indication that she was interested in me. I sat there frozen while Trisha scurried down the bleachers and disappeared through the doorway, ending the moment. She had done what she wanted to do, and I was okay with it. I felt a rush of adrenaline as I gazed across the gym floor with my mouth hanging open in disbelief. Chris' laughter broke my trance. He was just as shocked that Trisha, arguably the most popular girl at school, had just kissed me for no apparent reason. And I had Chris and Jeff as my two witnesses!

That first kiss made a lasting impression on me. I started noticing more things about girls that piqued my interest. It seemed like my neighborhood became littered with cute girls overnight. My brother James and I would stay up late into the night talking about them. Girls scared both of us. Most of our apprehension about talking to girls came from our poverty. Our reality extinguished any sparks of confidence or self-esteem necessary to approach girls. The kiss from Trisha removed a layer of barriers that blocked me from venturing too far into the minefield of sexual thoughts. My curiosity and discussions with classmates about sex consumed an inordinate amount of my time. Unfortunately, I wasn't able to have meaningful conversation with my dad about sex, primarily due to the 62-year age difference between us. What he faced in 1918 was drastically different from my experiences in 1980. Any discussions I had on the topics were with my brothers and classmates or from something I inferred from the neighbor's stash of dirty magazines strewn around his house.

One of my classmates, Charlene, also lived in my neighborhood. I knew Charlene had a crush on me, but I never had the courage to act on it. Charlene was a pretty girl. Her yellow skin was clear and free of the acne that most of us dealt with constantly. Even though she was a grade behind me in school, she was tall for her age and fully developed physically. Her breasts were larger than most of the other girls, and they attracted the attention of most people in the neighborhood, even grown men. When we played in the field across from my aunt's house on First Street, she usually wore tight nylon shorts. They showed off her big legs and cute shape!

Charlene and I played together a lot in the field across from my Aunt Rosie's house. Even though she didn't resemble the tomboys at school, she would still chase me anyway and didn't hesitate to play rough or try to tackle me. Her family loved to fish, so we used to catch grasshoppers for freshwater fishing in Municipal Park. Over time our playing evolved, and she started bumping into me and holding onto me for a few seconds—long enough for me to get aroused. It was embarrassing for me, but Charlene thought it was funny. Once she discovered how to trigger my arousal, she never let a day go by without getting me worked up.

One day, Charlene was extra flirty, and from the time I arrived at the park she started tugging, teasing, and hugging on me until I was aroused. She usually waited until the end of the day when the sun was setting to begin her teasing touches, just before it was time to go inside before dark. However, this day was different. It was early evening. I didn't have the growing shadows to hide the bulge in my shorts. As always, my embarrassment started mounting. Just as I was about to run home, Charlene made me the proposition of a lifetime.

"If you stay outside and play, I will teach you about a girl's body!" she said. She must have seen doubt on my face because she added a resounding, "I promise, I will."

Even though I was skeptical, she really didn't have to ask twice. There was absolutely no way I was going to miss this opportunity with her. I had only seen parts of the female anatomy in my neighbor's dirty magazines, so I agreed with a resounding "YES!"

An unprecedented level of awkwardness filled the air as Charlene and I waited for the evening sun to diminish a bit further. We didn't run and play as much as we usually did. I was amped up with anticipation, and my arousal wasn't going anywhere. As the sun slowly set behind the tree line, it was finally time to carry out the scene I had been rehearsing in my mind from the moment she made her proposition.

That's when Charlene added a twist that caught me by surprise. She would only show me unclothed parts of her body from a distance, and I couldn't touch her. That was drastically different from what I had been imagining. I pleaded with her to let me see them up close. Despite my efforts, she wouldn't budge. I was in no position physically or mentally to bargain. I reluctantly agreed to her last-minute deviation. After all, it still meant I'd get my first peek at a real woman's unclothed body, even from a distance. I was going to take what I could get.

She convinced me that I'd get a great view if she sat in the large oak tree that we often played in. There was a large horizontal branch on it, eight feet from the ground. It was sturdy enough to hold ropes and makeshift swings that my brothers and I had played on years earlier. Near the end of the branch, there was a Y-shaped split where Charlene planned to sit. She could easily pull her stretchy shorts to the side and I could get a good look. She climbed into the tree and methodically straddled the branch, her bottom perfectly filling the Y-shaped opening where the branch split.

"Close your eyes until I'm ready!" Charlene called down from the tree.

I was emotionally spent from the minutes of torture, so I robotically followed her instructions and closed my eyes. She seemed to be taking forever. I wanted to peek ahead of time. However, I didn't want to risk squandering the opportunity, so I kept my eyes tightly shut as promised, patiently waiting for her to give me the okay to look.

Charlene started slowly counting down from ten as I waited underneath her. Just as she reached zero, I opened my eyes to a flood of warm liquid splashing me in my face and eyes! I gasped for air, inhaling some of the liquid through my nose. More startled than anything else, I stumbled on the uneven ground underneath the tree. My clothes and hair were drenched in what I quickly figured out was Charlene's urine. My eyes and sinuses burned from her cruel trick. I could hear Charlene laughing uncontrollably as I slowly collected my bearings enough to start walking towards my house. Her trick worked perfectly, and I was gullible enough to get a golden shower without ever seeing her unclothed body.

Why is this story relevant? Unless you are intimately familiar with growing up in an impoverished environment, it's easy to overlook many of the immediate and long-term hazards that lie within. Yes, it's funny now to think about how gullible I was to let Charlene execute her dirty trick to perfection, but the narrative could have been drastically different. If Charlene had offered to have sex with me, I would have accepted her offer with complete certainty. At the time, I knew essentially nothing about sex, and I surely wouldn't have worn protection. In the few years following Charlene's trick on me, she had three children by three different guys, had dropped out of high school, was addicted to crack cocaine, and had turned to a life of prostitution to support her habit. I would have likely been the father of one of her children and been caught up in the middle of her complex quandary. She was in no condition to parent any of her children. Knowing that my dad raised us to take ownership of our responsibilities and for the decisions we made, it would have created an incredibly difficult terrain for me to navigate.

Once I got home that night, I reflected on the sequence of events and was disappointed that I let my raging hormones totally overwhelm my common sense. Despite numerous warning signs that the situation was veering off course, I let my emotions get the best of me. In most scenarios, our lives are usually not drastically defined by one good decision or one bad decision. It is usually a combination of making decisions a certain way that defines who we are. However, some one-time decisions can have significant implications. My dad never found out about the dirty trick and, fortunately, Charlene didn't tell anyone either. Despite Charlene's repeated requests to meet up again, her deception ended our after-school rendezvous and added to my fear of girls. But it also saved me from a regrettable alternative.

Risky Business

Once we hit our early teens, in a change of pace from our norm of avoiding contact with girls, James and I started smiling at Thelma, a nice girl in our neighborhood who constantly walked up and down the street in front of our house. She appeared to be in her early 20's but she was only 16, the same age as James, though we never saw her at school. At the time, neither one of us really knew why she spent so much time walking back and forth in the evenings and at night. I didn't know where she lived. I only knew that she spent a lot of time walking to and from someone's house at the end of my street. There were periods of time when she wouldn't come through for several weeks, and I never knew where she went when she disappeared. Then, suddenly, she'd be back walking the street every day for a couple of weeks.

Over a period of several months, Thelma became friendlier with us. She even slowed down to talk to us sometimes as she walked. She took a predictable walking pattern through the neighborhood, so I planned activities in my front yard to coincide with her late evening trips past the front of my house. One evening just as it was starting to get dark, Thelma came to the edge of my yard to talk. I was nervous around girls, but we'd formed a certain familiarity smiling and waving at each other over a period of time. In this seemingly inevitable encounter in my yard, Thelma was even easier to talk with than I imagined. She flirted heavily. With zero control over my hormones, I had to quickly put both hands in my pockets to hide the embarrassment that was quickly forming.

"Have you ever had sex before?" she asked without any hesitation.

"No," I quietly admitted, even though I wanted to lie.

"Well, if you want to have sex with me, be outside near the corner of your house tomorrow night when I come through," she whispered before walking away.

I fully intended to be there, ready to go, even though I had no experience or first-hand knowledge of sex. Months of coy looks, waves, and flirting with Thelma was going to culminate the next day. I didn't sleep that night and could hardly wait to get home from school the next day.

After a long day at school, I rushed home with anticipation of my rendezvous at the corner of my porch with Thelma. As I paced around the yard, waiting for the sun to go down, Thelma walked by several times, as she usually did during the daylight. My neighbor, Horton Williams, was also working in his yard. He had noticed my increasing communication with Thelma. He was a cool guy who kind of looked out for my brother James and me at certain times when we were younger. Horton came over and started with his normal greeting.

"What's happening, Ronnie?"

"Not too much. Just about to go in the house." I replied quickly, not wanting to get into a long conversation since the sun was starting to go down.

He didn't seem to buy my simple response and started to probe a little deeper.

"I see you watching Thelma a lot and talking to her sometimes when she walks through. You need to be careful with her," he warned.

I was embarrassed to admit that I had indeed been talking with her, but there wasn't much to hide since she walked in front of both our houses constantly. Even as Horton and I were talking, Thelma made another trip down the street.

I wanted the conversation to end quickly, but I also wanted to know why I needed to be careful.

"What do you mean 'be careful with her'?" I asked.

"I know what you're thinking, but you can't have sex with her," he said. "Some girls you can have sex with and some girls you can't." I still didn't understand, and I was ready to wrap up the conversation before the sun went down. He could tell I didn't get it.

"Look, Ronnie, you are a good kid. Thelma is a prostitute and I heard she has crabs," Horton declared. "If you have sex with her, you're going to get the crabs too. They'll make you scratch like a mangy dog for a week and your balls are going to swell up like Washington apples. It's going around bad nowadays and even the medicine won't kill them!"

I didn't know anything about sex, STDs, or condoms, but I knew I didn't want the crabs. Needless to say, I hid from Thelma from that point forward. I believe Horton had a conversation with her because she eventually stopped walking down the street. Horton's last-minute conversation saved me from what I didn't know. Because of his intervention, I avoided having sex with Thelma. He didn't have to warn me, but he knew more than I did and was willing to get involved to keep me from making a mistake. I appreciated that. By heeding his warning, I learned another valuable lesson about sex and potential consequences. The right type of intervention can be highly effective, without a person actually having to endure the negative repercussions!

#stayingSTDfree, #positiveintervention, #sexeducation

What Lies Beyond the Cul-De-Sac?

One of the reasons I didn't progress faster in my life was my lack of confidence. I was afraid to step up, explain my situation, and ask for help. Since I didn't have exposure to the elements of a better life, I didn't know what I didn't know. Most of the people who did know better weren't reaching out to help me.

My life closely resembled that of a person confined to living in a cul-de-sac. A cul-de-sac is a dead-end street with a circle at one end for turning around. You can't keep going; you can only turn back the way you came. People who live in a closed environment don't know what they don't know. Being limited to the confines of a closed environment limits their potential. We need to mentally get out of the cul-de-sac to see things differently. Helping others isn't just about giving them a job or money. Helping can be about imparting wisdom that you have so someone else can benefit from it and move along the spectrum of knowledge. Acting to help educate others is even more valuable than giving them money. It is analogous to helping a hungry person learn to fish rather than simply giving them a fish. Hidden Gems need someone to expose them to a better way of life, one that they can see and physically touch, or they may never realize what lies beyond the cul-de-sac. To grow, we all need to get out of our comfort zone, mentally and physically, and learn the things we don't know. It takes courage and curiosity aimed in the right direction. We must learn to question the status quo rather than living only by what we've experienced. #openminded, #nostatusquo, #teachtofish

The Turning Point in My Life

Sometimes we get a wake-up call to help us change course. For me, it occurred at the end of middle school during the most turbulent period of my pre-adult life. It was an age when many kids fully embraced and exercised their bullying tendencies. They took every opportunity to embarrass kids who showed any signs of weakness. Although I wasn't weak, I was extremely shy and quiet. I also had tons of potentially embarrassing issues lurking in every crevice of my life. As a result, I pretty much stayed to myself, except for a few friends. I was constantly walking on eggshells to avoid exposing anything that might be used against me later.

Like many kids around that age, I wasn't mentally equipped or mature enough socially to handle many of the insults from my childhood bullies. When kids laughed at me, the embarrassment would cause my already fragile self-esteem to nosedive even further. My protection mechanism would kick in and I'd go into a shell, sometimes for weeks at a time. I didn't know of another viable shield to guard against the verbal insults besides avoiding the perpetrators.

Staying in protection mode was detrimental to my psyche. Unfortunately, my tendency at the time was to automatically use the alone time to perpetually diminish my self-worth. In the solitude, I easily identified factors that I believed separated me from the other kids. One obvious divider was financial. On the surface, it appeared that we were poorer than most people in the neighborhood. The cool kids showed off their new, expensive Jordache and Calvin Klein jeans with K-Swiss, Penny Loafers, or Hush Puppies shoes. My clothes came from the local Goodwill thrift store. On rare occasions, we shopped at Roses, a local discount department store. Once, my dad surprised me with a pair of Converse All-Star sneakers. My brother Gerald showed me how to use a tire brush and bleach to make them white as snow. In some ways, it made me feel like the other kids!

As puberty kicked in, the acne on my face bloomed like an azalea bush in spring. It contributed to my extreme shyness and low self-esteem. As early as the seventh grade, I was essentially a recluse and in a dark place at school. I had poor hygiene, which was magnified during the winter months as temperatures dropped below freezing and we could heat only part of our house. We never had indoor plumbing or a bathtub; just water stored in recycled milk jugs from the neighbor's outdoor faucet. It was used for drinking, cooking, and also to wash under my arms and private areas. It was not uncommon for me to go several days without taking a bath. Some summer months were just as bad. I struggled with severe mosquito bites. There was something about my blood that they loved. I couldn't resist scratching to the point that I had open sores covering most of my legs. The ones that healed over time left scars and dark circles. Some of the kids joked that I was rich because I had coins all over my legs.

In school, I struggled to complete schoolwork during the short, designated class periods, and I fell behind. This, coupled with my poor study habits and innate procrastination, exacerbated my below-grade-level status. Teacher assessments and placement tests relegated me to slower-paced remedial classes for all of my core subjects. I needed more time to digest the information because I couldn't read at a regular pace. By the time I reached the eighth grade, I was on the verge of failing every class.

In contrast, my life outside of school was vibrant and exciting. I spent a great deal of my free time working in our garden, doing mechanic work on cars, and hunting for scrap metal to earn extra cash. I also loved experimenting with everything from making moonshine to making a cannon using homemade gunpowder. For this reason, I didn't value school or grasp how bad my school situation was.

Even with only a couple of weeks remaining in class, homework remained low on my priority list. I always had more interesting work to do at home after school and on weekends. Attending school was a necessary evil that I had to endure. My dad told me I could legally quit school once I turned 16 years old. He was hopeful that my perspective would change. However, at the time, 16 couldn't come fast enough. I wasn't able to connect the dots that by doing my boring homework, it would somehow result in an improvement to my poor living conditions. I was in survival mode, hustling to earn cash to supplement my dad's $190 a month Social Security check.

As the school year came to a close, my overall perception of middle school was not good. Sports and the few friends I had who didn't make fun of me didn't outweigh the barrage of teasing jokes and insults that I endured from other students. Additionally, my teachers had overcrowded classes and no time to deal with my level of shyness or to adjust assignments to accommodate for my work requirements outside of school. As a student, I was in no-man's land and fell between the cracks of the boilerplate teaching approach. Teachers often criticized me openly in front of the class for not completing homework. That gave the classroom goons a readily available source of insults to use against me. This vicious cycle cemented my feelings of inadequacy.

I made it through most of the summer after the eighth grade, ignoring the fact that I had failed math and English. I knew I had failed, but I hadn't taken any action to rectify the failures. I used the summer to earn money for the household by doing extra work at Twin M Farms picking peas, cucumbers, and corn, and doing mechanic work which included rebuilding a few car engines. I didn't realize that, because of my failures, I was required to attend summer school in order to advance to high school until one particular weekend near the end of the summer. I was talking with my friend Dewark Warrington when he mentioned being relieved about almost finishing summer school. I was surprised. Even though I had not seen him most of the summer, I didn't realize it was because he had also failed classes and was making them up over the summer. At that moment, it hit me that I also should have been in summer school, making up the failed classes along with Dewark and other kids.

My anxiety built at a rapid rate as I finally realized the predicament that I was in. With no other option, I had to tell my dad what happened. By then, my dad was legally blind, suffered from bleeding ulcers, and leaned heavily on me to be responsible for myself. I had even been driving for several years by then. I felt ashamed on multiple levels to be failing school. He trusted me to act responsibly, and I had done a poor job of upholding his trust in me due to my carelessness. He had taught me to take care of issues and handle my business on my own before anyone had to ask or require me to do so, but this time I fell down on the job.

As tension continued to build throughout that night, I started processing the embarrassment of failing the eighth grade. While all my friends would pass on to high school, I would be left behind, stuck in middle school. I also reflected on all the reminders about summer school and warning signs that I somehow failed to catch. I couldn't have been more frustrated by my carelessness. I had no one to blame but myself. So, I decided to make a conscious effort to try to save myself.

We didn't have a car at the time, so before daybreak the next morning I was on my bicycle taking the six-mile ride down to Sidney Phillips Middle School, the summer school location, to see if they could help me. I made it there just as the morning tardy bell sounded. There were hundreds of kids hurrying to classes and excited about enjoying the remaining days of the summer.

I was neither polished nor rehearsed in ways of talking to adults or handling serious affairs. I swallowed hard as I approached the front reception desk.

"Ma'am, can you please help me go to summer school?" I asked the receptionist, in my normal fast speech and sheepish voice.

There was a silence in the office. As my dad would say, it was so quiet that you could hear a rat pissing on cotton. After the long silence, the office worker made no effort to hide the disbelief on her face.

"What do you mean, 'Can I help you go to summer school?'" she replied, purposely saying it loudly enough for the others in the office to hear her. "Summer school is almost over! There are only three days left!" she said.

Her words immediately took my breath away. Tears streamed down my face as quickly as they could form in my eyes. It was confirmation that I had to repeat the eighth grade. My oversight and lack of focus had changed the course of my life forever. In one last act of desperation, I threw my shyness and pride out the window and begged the lady to help me. I got a resounding "NO" with every attempt I made. My poor study habits and procrastination had caught up with me. The stigma associated with flunking out of middle school was harsh. I'd be reminded of it throughout high school because I'd be a year behind the same classmates who had passed the eighth grade during the year I had failed.

After reluctantly accepting the fact that I had failed, the tears continued to stream down my face as I begrudgingly made my way back outside to my bicycle. There was a long and sad ride ahead of me. As I got on my bicycle, I realized the front wheel was severely warped. In my haste to get to the school, I sped down a steep hill. Just before I reached the school, I had hit the edges of several sidewalks. The front wheel of my bicycle was bent too severely to ride. So, to add insult to injury, I had to push my bike the entire six miles back to Mobile Terrace.

It was another restless night. I replayed the morning's events over and over in my mind, promising myself that I would never be in the same situation again. While I was out in the yard replacing the wheel on my bike the next morning, my dad felt his way to the side door of our house and called for me to come over. He sensed the pain I was going through and suggested I ride over to my old school and ask the principal if he could help. It sounded like a long shot, but I rode over to Hillsdale Middle School anyway. Luckily, Mr. Long, the principal, was there with most of the staff, preparing for the next school year. He remembered me as I approached, and I immediately started pleading my case. He couldn't believe I had almost let the entire summer pass without asking about summer school, but he also could hear the desperation in my voice and sense that my situation was dire.

"Ronnie, let me see what I can do," he said. "I'll call the principal at Sidney Phillips to see if he'll agree to let you take the final exams for math and English. It's not likely that he will allow it, but I'll ask. Also, you haven't learned anything since school ended so it's even less likely that you'd pass the final exams."

I could hardly believe what I was hearing! I thought I was dead in the water regarding summer school, and his words were a lifeline I never thought I would catch. I had one last chance to pass the eighth grade. I seized the moment and couldn't stop thanking him! I hopped on my bike and rode home to tell my dad the good news. In my mind, I took Mr. Long's response as a resounding "YES" to my taking the final exams. I still had to pass the tests, but at least I had a glimmer of hope. When I told my dad what happened, he was proud of me for talking with Mr. Long on my own, for being honest, and, in the process, feeling a sense of accomplishment when things didn't seem possible. I could have lied and said I didn't receive any paperwork about summer school. However, my dad always taught me to be honest, to own up to my mistakes, and to do my best to make things right.

It was a third sleepless night, and I was up and out of the house bright and early the next morning! As I started the six-mile trek back to Sidney Phillips, I was careful to not hit the curbs on the sidewalks head-on like I had on the last trip. With all my shyness seemingly gone overnight, I confidently approached the same receptionist. Her face held the same shocked look that it wore during our last meeting.

"I already told you that you failed, so what are you doing back here again?" she asked defiantly.

I let her know that I had the approval to take the final exam in both classes, and then I asked to speak to the principal. She directed me to sit in the office until the principal returned from making his rounds. Deep down inside, even I didn't believe it was fair to simply take the final exams without attending summer school like other students had. However, I convinced myself that passing the finals would mean I did earn my way to high school.

As the minutes slowly ticked by on the clock, I tried my best to think of every lesson, comment, and example my teachers ever made. When the principal arrived, I was pleasantly surprised by his friendliness.

"So, you're Mr. Stallworth?" he said with a smirk on his face. "Mr. Long called me about you. You think you got a chance of passing the final exams?" he continued, raising his eyebrows.

I quickly spoke up. "Yes sir, I'm going to do my best. I don't want to fail the eighth grade and get left behind."

He seemed eager to walk me to the English classroom for the first final, but I felt he thought I would fail. The receptionist stared at me as if she wanted to call out, "Dead man walking!" The principal introduced me to the class as Mr. Stallworth as I stood face to face with students I'd never seen before. I sat in one of the few vacant seats in the front of the class. It was the last day of summer school, and there was no time for me to be passive or indecisive. I had a job to do.

I diligently cranked through the English final exam as soon as the paper hit my desk. It took several minutes for my hands to stop shaking. My paper was wrinkled because my palms were sweaty with anxiety. The exam was as stressful as it could get. Almost as quickly as it started, the teacher said "Time's up! Put your pencils down and pass your papers to the front of the row!"

I was done. The teacher escorted me to the math classroom for the next final exam. As I had done on the English exam, I dove right in. I struggled to remember bits and pieces of what I'd learned throughout the year. One by one, I worked as many of the problems as I could. When I finished, I said a big prayer and thanked the teachers and the principal for giving me a chance to take the final exams. I even thanked the receptionist, who gave me one last look of disapproval as I walked out of the building.

When I made it back home, my dad said he was proud of me for doing my best. He understood it was going to be difficult for me to pass; he did his best to temper my expectations. I spent the rest of the day working in our vegetable garden in the field behind our house and feeling somewhat content that I had at least given it my best shot on the finals.

The next morning, I rode my bike back over to Hillsdale Middle School to thank my principal, Mr. Long, for his help. He was a nice man who cared about the kids. As I walked up to the front doors of the school, Mr. Long greeted me at the door.

"You did it, Ronnie! You passed both finals! You will be at Baker High School as a ninth grader this fall," he said before I could even get the words "thank you" out of my mouth. I was in total shock; this news meant the world to me. Tears of joy sprang to my eyes. I hugged Mr. Long and everyone else in the office before I took off, rushing home to tell Dad the good news.

My dad was so proud of me, and I was equally proud of his guidance. Rectifying the classroom failures, procrastination, and missed details that almost caused me to fail the eighth grade forced me to face my fears and break through my shyness. My dad taught me to be honest with myself and others, even when telling a lie might seem easier. By doing things the right way, with integrity, I'd be able to feel success firsthand from my diligence. He knew I had the ability to be successful, but I couldn't remain stuck in the shy and passive state of mind. He also knew that I'd have to figure out how to balance competing priorities and sacrifice my pride and fears to improve and achieve my objectives. I carried immense pride and joy in my heart for the remainder of the summer.

This was a turning point in my life! I swore I would never be in that situation again. I had overcome most of my shyness. I learned to read full sentences that summer. I dodged a bullet by narrowly passing the eighth grade and was on my way to high school with my classmates. The shy and illiterate Ronnie, who hid who he truly was and wasn't living up to his potential, was gone for good. A more confident, assertive, and driven young man emerged. #owningmyresponsibilities, #wordshurt, #setbacksarenotpermanent, #keeplearning, #treatpeoplefairly

☀ **Words of Wisdom** ☀
"Setbacks are not the same as failures, and failures are not final unless you give up. Don't stop after a setback."
-Ronnie Stallworth, Sr.

SECONDARY LESSONS

After barely scraping through the eighth grade, I moved on from Hillsdale Middle School with a completely different outlook on school. My new focus was on becoming a more proficient reader, paying attention in class, and completing homework assignments to the best of my ability. I was determined to never be on the verge of repeating a grade level in school again. This mindset shift propelled me to strive for higher grades. However, I didn't have the skillset to perform at a higher level when I first reached Baker High School.

I was used to the pace of remedial classes in middle school. Remedial courses were taught at a slower pace to allow students like me more time to absorb the course material. When I started the ninth grade, I was in all regular-paced classes. I initially underestimated the faster pace, but my heightened focus in the classroom and dedication to completing homework helped me earn average grades starting in the second quarter of my freshman year. In one of my classes, Alabama History, I was so fascinated by the content that my goal was to make a perfect score in the class. My interest in history progressively grew in the class primarily because it helped me understand many of the tough situations my dad had to endure, such as Jim Crow laws and Governor George Wallace's hatred toward Black people. My attention and effort did not go unnoticed by my teacher, Mr. Sutherlin. He saw it as a sign of maturity and said he was no longer going to call me Ronnie. He wanted to give me a more grown-up name. Mr. Sutherlin was the first person to start calling me Ron, and I liked the grown-up name change!

In high school, I was reunited with my brother James. He was two grade levels ahead of me in school, and by the time I arrived at Baker High School, James had established himself as a capable student in the eyes of most teachers and administrators. James was smart and athletic. The head football coach, Coach Oden, and his assistant, Coach Richmond, marveled at his athleticism during physical education classes. Both coaches constantly courted James to try out for the school football team. However, he had never tried out for or played organized sports. Other students were also impressed by James's athleticism. I benefited from his popularity from the moment I arrived at Baker High School as "James's Little Brother."

I was also athletic and played freshman basketball and football. James and I dreamed about playing professional football and following in the footsteps of one of our distant cousins, John Stallworth, who played for the Pittsburgh Steelers. I enjoyed playing both sports but eventually gave up football and focused on only basketball.

By June 1982, I had completed the ninth grade at Baker High School. As my dad had predicted earlier, my maturity and drive for continuous improvement had ramped up, and I no longer wanted to quit school when I turned 16 years old. In fact, I was more motivated than ever to prove myself academically. I had passed all my freshman classes and, although I wasn't required to attend summer school, I attended anyway with the objective of graduating high school early. It was a vastly different approach for me, with much loftier aspirations than in previous years. Going to summer school also had the added benefit of completing World History, a sophomore course, during the eight-week summer session versus taking it during the regular school year for nine grueling months with Mrs. Cramer. She had the reputation of being the toughest teacher at Baker High School. Going to summer school after the ninth grade was a win–win scenario for me.

That summer unfolded as planned. I completed World History and started my sophomore year in a much better position than in previous years. Athletically, I focused solely on basketball, and as for James, Coach Oden and Coach

Richmond finally convinced him to play football for the school team his senior year. It was a learning experience for James and an adjustment to taking on more criticism. In one instance, Coach Oden scolded James as the team sat around watching video footage from the previous football games.

"Stallworth!" he'd yell to James, "I'm sick of you wearing brown socks during the game! You need to get white socks like the rest of the team!"

The reality was we couldn't afford to buy socks. He was actually looking at James' brown legs. We were tempted to correct him but decided it would only bring more unwanted attention. We let Coach Oden go on believing James was wearing brown socks.

James and I viewed making the Baker High School teams as a key step to accomplishing our goals of one day playing sports professionally. When we shared the news with Dad about me making the Baker High School basketball team and James making the football team, Dad was ecstatic even though he didn't fully understand the scope or magnitude of our goals.

"That's great!" he said. "I'm really proud of both of you. Will they pay you a lot of money?"

It was funny to us at the time that he thought we'd get paid for playing high school sports. I knew it was because we had it tough financially and he was yearning to see us have a better life. Unfortunately, he was completely blind by 1982 and never got to actually see us play.

Life at Baker High School was continuing to improve. Although James had never played organized sports before his senior year of high school, he was so dominant that he had a number of Division I university scholarship offers. We both completed the school year as top athletes. James graduated from Baker High School in May 1983 and decided to accept a football scholarship at Southern University in Baton Rouge, Louisiana. Shortly after starting his first quarter of school, he became homesick and decided to return home to reassess his career path. At that point, neither one of us had spent time away from Mobile. He worked odd jobs for about six months before giving football another try at Alabama State University in Montgomery. He performed well on the football field and in the classroom that fall, but after a few months of college life, he made the decision to leave Alabama State University and move back home permanently. That was his last attempt to play college football.

I was a standout basketball player my tenth-grade year, but Baker High School was more known for their baseball team. Basketball and football didn't receive as much attention. Therefore, after my tenth-grade year, I decided to attend a different high school that had a more established basketball program. It was a good time for me to switch schools since James had already graduated. I looked at several schools in

Mobile. After considering the logistics, I decided to transfer to Murphy High School. I had cousins, David and Mary Stallworth, who lived in that school district, and they agreed to let me stay with them occasionally and use their address. Using my cousins' address was a way to work around the school district restrictions to only attend a school in your district.

By working odd jobs and selling aluminum cans I saved up enough money to buy an old car from Horton Williams' dad. It was a 1974 Toyota Celica that I purchased for $400. He agreed to let me pay him $200 down and pay the remainder over a 6-month period. His leniency worked out great for me, and the car got me back and forth to Murphy High School from Mobile Terrace where I was still living with my dad and James. #learnfrommistakes, #changeofscenery, #loftiergoals

Farewell, Father

After James returned from Southern University, he and I were reminiscing one night about the success we were having in sports. It was November 9, 1983, and we were really feeling like our lives were on the upswing. Shortly after my conversation with James, I was staring at the ceiling thinking about the next phase of my life and what I needed to do to continue improving and growing. I was having trouble falling asleep and could hear my dad's heavy breathing. It wasn't his normal snoring, so I decided to check on him.

"Dad?" I said, touching his arm lightly. There was no response.

"Dad?" I asked again as I shook his arm a little harder than the first time. Still no response.

"Dad!" I yelled loud enough to wake up anyone that was sleeping, shaking him even harder. Nothing.

With a sense of urgency, I jumped up, flipped the light switch on and woke up James. Together, he and I shook Dad's body, yelling multiple times for him to wake up. We tried desperately to wake up Dad, but he was unresponsive, even though he was breathing heavily through his open mouth.

My brother Michael lived next door. I ran out of the house to his bedroom window and started knocking to wake him up. It was about 1:00 AM. Michael appeared at the window, half-dressed.

"What's wrong?" he yelled.

"It's Dad," I shouted. "He's not waking up!"

Michael and I ran back to the house where our dad was still unconscious but breathing. Michael picked up Dad's body as if he were a child and carried him outside to our truck. We quickly drove to Springhill Memorial Hospital. As we sat inside the waiting room, the three of us started reflecting about the impact Dad had on each of us. Seeing him in the hospital was terrifying. Still, we all had expectations that he would be okay. We all saw him as invincible.

As the doctor emerged from the intensive care unit, he didn't have a positive look on his face. Based on his assessment, our dad wouldn't make it much longer. It was surreal news; we couldn't believe it. We stayed in the waiting room for hours, expecting the doctor to tell us things had improved, and he'd be okay. After waiting at the hospital for 48 hours, James and I left for a couple of hours to get food. When we returned to the hospital, the nurse stopped us at the entrance and told us she was glad to see us because our dad had made a remarkable recovery. She said he was laughing and joking with the nurses and back to his normal self. James and I looked at each other with a big sigh of relief. Her words validated our original thinking that Dad was indestructible. Her words were fantastic to hear.

James and I quickly went back to his room to tell him about the scare he had given us. Unfortunately, we learned that his condition had not changed. He was still in his bed with a breathing tube. We returned to the nurses' station to ask about his condition.

"Oh, I'm so sorry," she said. "It wasn't Mr. Stallworth that I was talking about earlier, it was Mr. Johnson. Mr. Stallworth's condition hasn't changed." James and I were devastated. The nurse apologized for her mistake. As much as we wanted to accept her apology, neither James nor I could digest the egregious error she made telling us that Dad had recovered.

More hours passed with no change in Dad's condition. Finally, the doctor asked Michael, James, and me to accompany him to Dad's room. My brothers and I stood together next to Dad as he took his last breath. He was gone.

Later, as Michael, James, and I exited the hospital, Michael asked me if I was old enough to take care of myself. I thought for a moment.

"Yes!" I said, sounding resolute. I knew it was my dad's prayer for years that God allowed him to live long enough for me to be able to take care of myself. Thankfully, God had done just that. At 16 years old, it was time for me to become a man. #losingahero, #bestdadever, #timetogrowup

Two-Door Studio

Life after Dad was tough. In our house, we still had no telephone, no plumbing, no toilets or shower. James and I were getting $194 a month total in social security survivors' benefits, and we used most of the money to pay the utility bills at the house—gas and electricity. My brother Gerald moved back into the house, and it caused the utility bills to skyrocket. The bill increased to the point we couldn't pay it. Eventually, all the utilities got disconnected for nonpayment, so I went most my junior year of high school without natural gas or electricity. We used candles to light the house at night.

A few times during that year, I remember returning home and seeing that the electricity was back on. One of my brothers learned how to hotwire electricity and turn it back on illegally. I occasionally saw unusual cars in the neighborhood near our house. I figured someone was looking to arrest us for stealing electricity. To avoid detection, I started parking behind the house in the woods. I would come in through the woods and enter through my back door and look out. On some occasions I would peek through the openings in the doorway and see people, including a deputy sheriff, looking to see if someone was in the house. So, we kept it dark to give the appearance of being completely abandoned. If I had been spotted, I probably would have been arrested as the culprit. I purposely avoided using anything electrical because deep down inside I knew it was stealing and I wanted to distance myself from it to the extent that I could, while still staying in the house. At the time, I had convinced myself that I didn't have any other viable place to live.

After several weeks of sneaking through the woods behind my house and entering through the back door, I noticed fresh stickers near the doorknob to contact the power company because they had questions. Within days, all utility connections were severed from the house. My brothers quickly moved out. James made another attempt at his college football career at Alabama State University, and Gerald moved in with one of his friends. I was living there alone.

Eventually, I would notice signs that someone had been walking around the back of my house. Utilities had been severed from the house, but they had not given up on finding the homeowner. The situation was dire, but I was determined to find a way to stay in the house that my dad built and raised us in. I had to come up with a plan to get in and out of the house without anyone noticing, so I created a trapdoor by cutting a hole in the floor in my bedroom and installing hinges. To get from the trapdoor to the back edge of the house without getting dirt on my clothes, I put roofing tin on the ground underneath the trapdoor. With this in place, I was able to go in and out by using the crawl space under the house, without going through either door. For the remaining months of my junior year, I parked my car in the woods and exited through the adjoining neighborhood using the trapdoor-and-roofing-tin route to remain undiscovered.

By my senior year, I'd had enough. Michael was living in California, Gerald was living part-time at the house but was in the process of moving, and James was pursuing his college football dreams. It was no way for me to live, so I accepted the fact that I would have to abandon the house that my dad put his heart and soul into building for us. I contacted my cousins again about living with them, since they lived in the Murphy High School district. I had already been using their street address to allow me to attend Murphy High School my junior year. Even though they welcomed me with open arms, I decided instead to move into my car for most of my senior year. I usually parked overnight in the Springhill Memorial Hospital parking lot in Mobile where my dad passed away. It was a well-lit area, so I didn't have to worry about any of the criminal activity that had cast a shadow over the prior two years. I had my clothes in my 1974 Celica. I took showers in the school locker room and washed my clothes in the washing machines near the gym for most of my senior year in high school.

We never had much money to live on, even when Dad was living. I was focusing on high school and playing basketball so there wasn't much time for work. With my junior year at Murphy High School being a transition year from Baker High School, I had made only a few friends at Murphy. To exacerbate the situation, I had been taking summer school classes to get ahead prior to transferring to Murphy High School, so by the time I started my senior year I was misaligned with other Class of 1985 students. I had already taken several senior-level courses the prior year with Class of 1984 students. The living arrangements in my car were not good. However, it was still better than the previous year living in the house with no electricity, no natural gas, and never having a telephone or bathtub. By comparison, living in my car really wasn't that bad. I had a small 8-inch television that plugged into my cigarette lighter, the car was fairly comfortable, and I could take a shower at Murphy High School before class.

As my senior year progressed, I considered my previous living situation in the house. It had become such a challenge and burden that the transition from the house to my car was relatively easy and seamless. It actually simplified my life by reducing my overall expenses and allowing me to be closer to Murphy High School. But with no one living in it, the house rapidly deteriorated. In many ways, it was a relief to no longer worry about the leaking roof, doing yard work, or dealing with the increasing number of rats and snakes in the house from the nearby woods. With that being the case, it was actually a much-needed relief to be living in the car. #livingontheedge, #guiltyaccomplice, #livinginfear

Mistaken for a Cool Kid

In high school, although I was a varsity athlete, I was not popular and still really struggled with confidence. I couldn't afford new clothes or to get haircuts on a regular basis. I couldn't even take showers other than at school. I didn't have many opportunities to improve my status. One thing that helped me gain popularity during my junior year was transferring from Baker High School to Murphy High School. Athletes at Murphy were regularly courted by Division 1 college scouts and were frequently in the news, which generated more clout for athletes on campus.

I was the same nerdy guy at Murphy that I had been at Baker. I carried a briefcase and had an afro. I was still a shy, quiet, and very polite kid. The modesty and humility instilled by my dad were still a huge part of my persona. Being on my own after my dad's passing turned me into a grown-up very quickly. While my maturity was keeping me alive, it wasn't exactly benefitting me around my peers in high school who were mainly focused on playing sports and chasing girls.

I was also more focused than ever before on my grades at Murphy High School, which solidified the nerd label. In some ways I was becoming more socially interactive. I made a new set of friends, and we spent more time together playing sports outside of school. I was more engaging and that was helping me overcome the geek identity. One night when I was still a junior, I received a major confidence boost and earned some popularity points just before one of our rival basketball games. We were playing McGill Toolen High School, one of the better schools in the area, in our home gym. McGill was a parochial school, about a mile away from Murphy.

As we dressed in our locker room, we could hear the crowd swelling outside the door. Our two campuses were historical rivals in athletics. This game was well-attended by fans from both schools. The winning school would earn bragging rights as well as the privilege of painting their school colors on one of the city's historical landmarks, a Civil War-era cannon located in the midtown area near both school campuses. Seniors on each team wanted to end their high school careers with a win against one of their hated rivals.

McGill was known for having some of the hottest girls in the city. Any time we ran into them around the city, boys were completely enamored by them. From my vantage point, the McGill girls who had come to the game to support their team were all out of my league. But at least they provided beautiful scenery.

There had been an intense pep rally earlier in the day to get our home crowd fired up. As game time approached, Coach Harris had us line up in the hallway outside the gym door. The girls' basketball teams always played each other ahead of the boys' varsity games. As we stood in the hallway waiting for the last few minutes of the girls' game to finish, a couple of my teammates spotted six beautiful girls from McGill walking toward us.

One of my teammates, Lawrence Finch, wasn't bashful at all. His nickname was "Little Lawrence" because he was the shortest guy on the team. Nevertheless, he was a smooth talker. He quickly strolled toward the small group of McGill girls and called out his favorite line.

"Hey little lady, what's your name?"

The girls giggled, looking at Lawrence as he tried to make small talk. That's when Craig, our teammate, walked over to provide support as Little Lawrence's wingman. In the gym, we could hear the crowd yelling and cheering. The girls' game was lasting longer than expected. Little Lawrence and Craig continued walking toward the six McGill girls, flirting hard and commanding their attention. It seemed as if they were going to get their digits. It took some smooth game for two guys like Little Lawrence and Craig to collect six McGill girls' phone numbers at once.

Then, out of nowhere, one of the girls in their group called out to me.

"Ronnie Stallworth! Is that you?"

It was always a surprise to me when I received any attention from girls. I was already nervous about the big game, and I was sure I had mistaken what I heard. Then Little Lawrence confirmed it.

"Stallworth, you know these girls?" Little Lawrence asked.

One of the girls stepped away from the group.

"Don't act like you don't know me," she said with a playful attitude.

She was Kendra Charleston, a beautiful girl I had gone to Baker High School with the year before. I remembered when I met her at Baker, she told me she had transferred from McGill. Kendra was attending that night's Murphy-McGill basketball game with some of her previous classmates even though she was now a student at Baker.

Kendra quickly came over and gave me a big hug right in front of all my teammates. That single hug put me on the map. Before then, the seniors in my classes looked down on me because I was an underclassman. Now these same seniors, my teammates, would be giving me high fives and talking me up outside the gym.

Little Lawrence and Craig could always get a girl's number. But for a McGill girl to walk away from them and come and hug me in front of everyone sent a statement— "Ronnie Stallworth was a ladies' man."

"Stallworth is friends with the hot girls from McGill!" Little Lawrence said, repeating the story to our other teammates. Suddenly, in the mind of my teammates, I knew all of the McGill girls, when in fact I knew only Kendra, and she didn't even go to McGill anymore.

I didn't correct them. Having that reputation was okay with me. After that confidence boost, I had a great game that night. My popularity blossomed overnight like a wildflower. For weeks to follow, several teammates treated me as if I was the star player on campus. It felt good for a nerd like me to be mistaken for a cool kid. It was easy to forget the lessons in humility I had learned from my father. It got to my head in ways that I would pay for later. In fact, there were setbacks around every corner to kill my momentum and put me back in my place. #mrpopularity, #coolpoints, #popularityisoverrated, #humilityisprime

☀ **Words of Wisdom** ☀
"Popularity is superficial; it keeps the focus on you.
Humility is superior; it requires you to
keep the focus on others."
–Ronnie Stallworth, Sr.

About a month after the game with McGill, we had an away game to play. The requirement was for us to meet at Murphy and all ride on the school bus together to the opponents' location. About a week before that game, I had picked up a small Sony Walkman while shopping at Goodwill and used it to play music. I usually isolated myself from the rest of the team, and it was a good way for me to relax. As I was sitting on the bus listening to music, Little Lawrence quickly grabbed my headphones and put them on his ears. I tried my best to shut off the Walkman before he heard the song playing but I was too late. Little Lawrence heard the song and immediately started laughing uncontrollably.

"This fool is listenin' to country music!" Little Lawrence yelled to everyone on the bus. There were a few seconds of silence and then everyone on the bus erupted into laughter. I was extremely embarrassed. A Black guy listening to country music was okay in the rural part of Mobile where Baker High School was located, but it was not going to get me any cool points at Murphy High School, which is in the city. I wanted to fit in at Murphy, so I pretended to like some of the popular hip hop and R&B songs that my Murphy peers listened to. However, my favorite music was country, and that's what I listened to privately. I had grown up on country music; I related to it better than any other music. When Little Lawrence caught me listening to Hank Williams Jr. that day on the bus, it killed most of the popularity momentum I had gained over the past few weeks. I was back to being a nerd again!

My senior year was a little better. I was one of the better players on the basketball team. That kept a few popularity points in my pocket. I had also gained enough confidence to have a few conversations with girls at school. One girl was really cute and caught my eye. Her name was Faith Keen. She wasn't flashy; she was naturally pretty without any makeup. I would smile at her in the hallway when we passed each other between class periods. She usually reciprocated with a smile of her own. Our hallway exchanges were awkward because she was also in my homeroom class. I never attempted to speak to her when she was sitting near me in homeroom. I could only manage a smile at her while in motion through the hallways. I really couldn't tell if she liked me or not.

One morning while walking into homeroom class, I took a chance and said hi to her. She didn't respond. I continued walking to my seat behind her. As other students trickled into the room, including several of her girlfriends, Faith turned around and looked at me. Her face wore an odd expression. It wasn't the friendly smile she usually flashed at me from the hallway. Still, I gave her a polite smile as I had always done.

With her girlfriends listening in, she asked, "Why do you always smile at me when we're in the hall?"

I was caught off guard. I wasn't expecting to have a conversation with her. In that moment, I could only think of speaking the truth.

"I was just being nice...and smiling," I answered.

A couple of the other girls started giggling. I could sense that they had been gossiping about me and my smiles at Faith in the hallway. I started to grow embarrassed.

"Don't be smiling at me because I've got a boyfriend," Faith said with a straight face. "He plays for Theodore High School. You see me wearing his jacket," she continued, with very little emotion. Faith's friends burst into laughter as she turned back around in her chair without saying another word.

In the hallways, I could quickly smile and keep walking without any response from her but in the classroom, I was forced to sit and take the brunt of her rudeness. When it came to high school embarrassments, this was the worst I had experienced—humiliation and public rejection from a pretty girl named Faith. #nerdagain, #countrymusiclover, #peerpressure, #innerbeauty

Positive Exposure

During my senior year, I was allowed to leave school early under a work-study program. I got a job working for an auto parts store, Nation Automotive. Thanks to my dad allowing me to work on cars, I quickly proved my value and was almost immediately promoted to supervisor. It was a great example of a parent teaching their kids a basic skill to use as an adult. #learnaskill, #valuecreation, #qualityparenting

💎 Gem Seeker Opportunity 💎

*Parents are often the first Gem Seekers that Hidden Gems encounter. **Even parents with little financial means can enrich their child's life by teaching them essential life skills they can use as an adult.***

The work-study program was a great fit for me because I was able to leave school early for work, and I learned a lot of real-life lessons in the class. The teacher, Mr. Stross, did an excellent job of commanding my attention. My appetite for learning had increased significantly by then and a good portion of the program focused on understanding finances. I keenly listened to anything related to financial literacy. To that point in my life, the only experience I had with finances and building wealth was to open a regular savings account and accrue the meager interest rate. I didn't have any exposure to investing beyond that.

Mr. Stross caught my attention with a challenge he made to the class one day. His proposition to the class was, "If you do what I tell you to do in this class, I'll show you how to invest $20 a week now and by the time you are 30 years old, you will have $100,000." I wasn't a mathematician but even I knew $20 a week times 52 weeks only equaled $1040 a year. For me to have $100,000 in only 13 years was mindboggling to me. His comment made me latch on to every word that exited his mouth.

By mid-term of my senior year, I needed only one credit to complete my high school graduation requirements. I could have graduated in December 1984, but the basketball season continued through the end of January 1985. I dropped one class so that I could remain on the basketball team through the end of the season without violating the school district's graduation policy. Once basketball season was over at the end of January, I asked to graduate even though there were still four months remaining in the school year. I never completed the second half of Mr. Stross' work-study class or learned his secret financial process. Even still, his comment, irrespective of the validity, was the first time I started thinking about building wealth from an investment perspective. #positiveexposure, #showmethemoney

Graduation to Real Life

I didn't bother attending the graduation ceremony in the spring of 1985. What mattered most to me was that I had finished high school. I knew my dad would be proud. Graduating from high school was a huge accomplishment. In the environment where I grew up, getting a diploma was an important, and often challenging, achievement. In my neighborhood at that time, many people hadn't graduated from high school. There were good, hard-working people in my neighborhood who had to drop out of school to work and support their families.

After graduation, I still hoped to play basketball in college. However, at that time I viewed working more hours at Nation Automotive and having an opportunity to progress into a higher-level managerial role as ranking higher on my priority list. The pay was not bad for an 18-year-old in my situation, and the store manager, Steven Dinkins, and assistant manager, Seth Gardner, went out of their way to teach me supervisory skills. The company also had regional and general manager opportunities, so the upside of working for Nation Automotive made it a viable career option for me at the time. The General Manager, Todd Mullins, convinced me that I had a bright future with the company, including the ability to one day take over his role, which motivated me even more! As a back-up plan, the working hours gave me the flexibility to still play basketball in recreational leagues with the hope of one day earning a walk-on scholarship at a major college.

By August 1985, I had developed a closer relationship with Seth Gardner. He helped me learn the details of managing the store and trained me as supervisor. I loved the job and moving to a supervisor role was a relatively seamless transition for me. I understood the automotive parts business intimately from the time I was 10 years old. Thanks to my dad giving me responsibility to run the watermelon stand on my own, I had developed the skill set and temperament to work with the public. Additionally, I made it a priority to let my direct reports know how much I appreciated them.

Seth and I had a great working relationship, and it eventually evolved to hanging out regularly after work as well. Seth introduced me to his mom, Olivia Gardner. She was a sweet lady who knew how to take charge of a situation when she needed to. Mrs. Gardner and I liked each other from our first meeting at her home. Although I visited their house once or twice a month, I didn't meet Seth's dad until later. When Seth came to work, he would routinely share one of his sandwiches with me. After a couple of weeks of sharing his lunch with me, he started bringing a whole extra lunch to work for me. It was actually from Mrs. Gardner being observant. She knew Seth wasn't eating two meals during lunch.

It was different being around the Gardners. They were a white, middle-class family, and I was from a poor Black neighborhood in the area and was still sleeping in my car. They always had food in their house. Their kitchen drawers and pantry were always full! It was something I had never seen before. My dad always made sure we never went hungry, but we rarely ever had extra food in our cabinets. Seeing that the Gardners had an abundance of food was exposure that I didn't forget. They cooked a steak one night. It was such a treat that I felt like I had arrived in life. I started cutting the steak all up into pieces to eat it. Mrs. Gardner stopped me.

"Ronnie, the best way to eat a steak is one piece at a time," she explained. "Only cut the piece you are going to eat." That lesson stuck with me. I felt privileged to be in such a nice environment. I appreciated learning how to conduct myself from people who knew better. I could sense that this would help me reach higher goals. The personal and career advice they gave me helped get me on a steeper learning curve with regard to personal development, continuous improvement, and striving for loftier goals. It was another example of someone knowing more than me and willingly sharing their knowledge in a way that I could digest and put to good use.

During one of our conversations, I shared with Mrs. Gardner that I was living in my car. She was shocked and immediately started helping me find an apartment. One of my colleagues, Scott Stevens, told us that his apartment complex was running a move-in special. The move-in special was to pay the first month's rent for November, and December would be half-off. In November 1985, I moved into the Dandale Court Apartments. Mrs. Gardner helped pay the first month's rent. I was so happy to have my own place, and it had a shower! I must have showered a half-dozen times a day the first few weeks. It was a game-changer for me, and it showed me I could do better than living in my car. Mrs. Gardner also showed me how to manage a budget. If I ran short of cash, she would help me get over the hump by paying for some items I bought at yard sales, but it was nothing elaborate. She didn't relieve me of the consequences of overspending my budget. She was a true Gem Seeker who provided me with positive exposure. It gave me a new perspective on life. The more I learned how to carry myself through environments where I felt uncomfortable, the more I wanted to live like the Gardners.

Mrs. Gardner took me to yard sales on Saturdays to buy items I needed for the apartment. She called it "going junkin'." Before this experience, I never understood that well-off people shopped at yard sales. Mrs. Gardner taught me how to manage money by showing me that buying used was just as good as buying new, but at 1/10th of the cost. Every Saturday was an adventure. We never knew what we'd find, and occasionally we'd get odd stares from homeowners. On one of our yard sale visits in a nice upper-middle-class neighborhood, the owner of the home pulled Mrs. Gardner aside to ask if she noticed the poor Black kid at the yard sale. The homeowner didn't realize she had brought me there. Mrs. Gardner was furious! I had never seen her get angry before.

"He's my son and I brought him here!" she told the homeowner of the yard sale. "Since you don't want him here, we'll both leave so you can take all of these items we picked out and sell them to someone else. Come on, Ron, we are getting out of here!" Mrs. Gardner shouted loud enough for everyone to hear. I was so happy that she defended me, and it created an even tighter bond between us. I knew she could be the boss when she needed to be.

After the move, I continued enjoying my job at the auto parts store. However, I still had the desire to play college basketball. I worked out at several gyms in town and played as much as I could to improve my skills. Although I had a tremendous amount of potential my senior year at Murphy High School, my scoring was only average. However, my field goal percentage, assists, and rebounds were fantastic. This was an indication that I needed to shoot the ball more and that my selfless play was actually hurting my chances of getting a scholarship. I remembered my coach yelling at me to shoot the ball and stop passing up shots. It was an example of me not applying myself even though I had the ability to do so. In order to impress college coaches, I would have to be more assertive, which required a shift from my comfortable, accommodating demeanor.

After showing my film and trying out at several schools, I received scholarship offers from a handful of smaller universities, including Jacksonville State University and several highly ranked junior colleges. But there were not as many Division I offers as I had hoped. I decided to continue working at Nation Automotive and hone my skills by playing over the summer with basketball players from Bishop State Community College, the University of South Alabama (also called USA or South), and other schools in the area. I performed well against the Division I players and even against some professional players, including Charles Barkley (Phoenix Suns), Terry Catledge (Orlando Magic), and other NBA players who used the University of South Alabama gym to keep in shape during the summers. My performance against them was validation for me that I could compete in Division I basketball and one day possibly play professionally in the US or overseas.

Another great spot for competitive pick-up games was in Atlanta. Many of the Atlanta Hawks basketball players frequented popular gyms for off-season pick-up games against other NBA and Division I players. Dominique Wilkins, Isaiah Thomas, Magic Johnson and other NBA players would be playing there to keep in shape during the off-season. They also had summer leagues going, and major college players could join in the mix. The NBA players were very particular to play only against high-quality competition to minimize the risk of getting injured. Many of them earned millions of dollars a year and couldn't afford to get injured.

I had set my target on playing at NC State University, and the additional time honing my skills had positioned me well to attempt to walk on and make the team. I was gaining more confidence and playing at a very high level. But during a city league basketball tournament in Mobile, I had an awkward fall and broke my right hand. As a right-handed shooter, it took several months before I could completely close my hand. During that time, I lost a lot of momentum. My college athletics dream was officially over.

Unsure of my next move, I started spending more time working. In addition to working at Nation Automotive, I was working three other jobs. I worked as a night-shift stocker at a Food World grocery store, I was a part-time youth basketball coach at the YMCA, and I worked in the paint and body shop at a local Toyota dealership. If my hours were short at the YMCA, I would teach an occasional aerobics class. In total, I was working more than 100 hours every week.

I yearned for a better lifestyle and poured every ounce of energy I had into working extra hours to accomplish that goal. Earning more money was a significant motivator, but I thoroughly enjoyed the work I was doing. Financially, the additional income and working hours improved my near-term quality of life. At the same time, a longer-term benefit was the expanded skillset and the level of respect I gained from my managers. Their recognition of my hard work and my mindset to earn my way to greater prosperity opened more doors for job promotions.

Recognizing my work ethic, Mrs. Gardner spoke with her husband, Jack, about hiring me at a local manufacturing plant where he was an HR manager. Mr. Gardner was initially opposed to hiring a recently homeless 19-year-old kid. His strategy was to hire people with families because they'd be less likely to resign, take off work

MOBILE PLANT

MOLECULAR SIEVES

randomly, or squander the opportunity because, unlike me, they had established responsibilities. His logic made sense and yielded the best success rate for new hires. Mrs. Gardner didn't care about his logic and insisted that he interview me, which happened in the summer of 1986. To my surprise, he asked only a few general questions during the official interview. My real interview had occurred weeks earlier when he came to Nation Automotive and acted as a disgruntled customer. Despite him acting overly irritated to see if I would break under pressure, I was cool and collected. He was impressed during the store visit and didn't see a need for a lengthy formal interview at the manufacturing plant. Shortly after the interview, I was informed that I was accepted for the Alabama Industrial Development Training (AIDT) class. It was an eight-week course to prepare me to work in a manufacturing plant. After completing the course in October 1986 and ranking #4 in the class out of 22 applicants, there was an economic downturn and hiring was delayed until the following March. My first day on the job was March 30, 1987, with a salary of $38,800. I now had an apartment and a great job, and I decided to buy a newer car. This time, I bought a used 1982 Nissan 280ZX.

The Gardners had changed my life! They were the ones who exposed me to a different way of living and thinking and helped accelerate my development and growth. Their investment in me was priceless. My confidence level was at an all-time high even after I had to give up my dream of playing college basketball. The manufacturing plant had an educational assistance program to pay for 80% of college tuition. It was a win-win situation for me. I was earning a great wage, and the company would practically pay for my education.

#applyinglessonslearned, #qualityfriendships, #takingachanceonme, #livelikethegardners, #unfairprofiling, #outofcomfortzone, #earnyourway, #strategicthinking, #thinkdetailstoo, #devilinthedetails, #movingonup

Three's a Crowd

Landing that job at the local manufacturing plant was a major step-change in my life. Step-changes are events that don't follow the normal growth trajectory we believe we're on. When I landed in that job, my life changed completely and immediately. I went from making minimum wage, working four jobs to get by, to essentially having one of the highest paying jobs in the area. My life was definitely on the upswing. Still appreciative of having indoor plumbing, I would take long, glorious showers, feeling washed over with a sense of accomplishment. I felt like I had finally arrived. I thought I was doing pretty well for myself. My steady income allowed me to buy a nice (used) sports car, new clothes, and things to spiff up my apartment. That all went to my head, and I began a subtle drift away from some of the core values my dad had instilled in me.

Even though I had limited experience with women during my formative years, my dad was relentless in teaching us to always treat people with respect—especially ladies. I had been raised to demonstrate humility and to think more about others than myself. Chivalry was alive and ever-present in our lives growing up. We learned to respect and show courtesy to women, and I always strived to live up to that standard. I didn't have the experience of growing up with my mom involved in my life, and my sister had passed away before I was born, but my dad did a great job of building a culture of respect for women in our household. Yet now that I had achieved some level of success, my focus was selfishly turning inward. My new status in life was a monumental change, and women were beginning to take notice. I soon found myself juggling three different young women who were all viable options for sharing quality time.

Two of the women were from my old neighborhood, and the third one was from a nearby city. Up to that point, I was a virgin. I had never even been with one woman, let alone tried to see three at the same time. I really didn't know what it felt like to be in a boyfriend/girlfriend relationship. My relationships with these women were mainly casual friendships with a lot of flirting. Still, only one of them knew there were others.

As my appearance continued to improve, so did my confidence. Getting regular haircuts, going to the gym, and driving a nice sports car around town made me feel pretty good about myself. As my conversations with each of the three young ladies continued, I was faced with the decision of whether to commit to one of them or continue down the path with all three. One of the women, Vernie Russell, wanted a commitment, but she wasn't who I really wanted to be with. The one I really wanted to be with, Dia Evans, was seeing another guy. The third woman, Eva Willis, lived in another city. I couldn't figure it out. I decided to go with the status quo and continued to see all three. I had the mindset that everything would somehow work out.

To be honest, it was a bit of a thrill for me. Getting so much attention from these women was a huge change of pace from how I had grown up. I had gone from being a virtual nobody in high school to now having three lady friends. Chris Warren, one of my friends from school who I hung out with from time to time, started referring to me as "Playa from the Himalayas." I had heard the phrase before but never directed toward me. The term was commonly used to describe a cool guy with a nice car who talked to several girls at the same time. On one hand, that was what my life looked like on the surface. On the other hand, it made me uncomfortable. It was never my intention to be a player; it wasn't how I was wired. At the time, though, I laughed Chris' label off as if it was a compliment. After all, there was this illusion that I was in a good situation! I wanted to sustain this illusion even though it conflicted with my values.

If Dia had been fully available, I probably would have immediately committed to her exclusively. She and I had history from Baker High School. Although I was a couple of years older than Dia, her parents really liked me. They knew my family and that I was a polite and respectful person. They thought I was going places in life. Her parents would ask me to come by occasionally to chat with them. In reality, it was Dia's mom's way of trying to hook us up.

Back in high school, I was really shy, and Dia was a little fast for me. After some back-and-forth and with prodding by her mom, I had built up enough courage to ask Dia to go to a movie. It was my senior year, and I had a part-time job to pay for our tickets. This was my first official date. When Dia agreed to go out with me, I spent a ton of time cleaning up my little Toyota Celica. To make things extra special, I bought her a nice card before I went to her house. When I arrived at her house to pick her up, Dia wouldn't come to the door. She'd had a change of heart and, after several minutes of my knocking, her mom came to the door to break the bad news—Dia didn't want to go to a movie with me. I couldn't believe it; I left heartbroken.

A couple of years passed before the next time I spoke to Dia. I was driving through the neighborhood in my fancy sports car when she flagged me down. That's how we reconnected. I wasn't the same shy kid I was back in high school. She apologized for her rejection back in high school, explaining that unbeknownst to me at the time, she had been seeing another guy. She admitted she felt I was too slow for her in high school. I didn't hold a grudge about the way she had treated me. In fact, her assessment of me in high school was probably accurate. But now that we had reconnected, Dia was even more beautiful than I remembered. I was open to asking her out again. The other guy she had been seeing in high school had broken up with her, and she was interested in talking to me.

As we rekindled our friendship, I told her about the other two women I was seeing. She was fine with it. She said she didn't want to be boyfriend/girlfriend. She still wanted to talk to other guys as well, which was fine with me, even though I did like her a lot. Balancing all these relationship dynamics was uncomfortable and out of character for me. However, I soon settled into a complacent mindset and convinced myself that it was okay to talk to all three women at the same time. I told myself the lie that being a "Playa from the Himalayas" wasn't such a bad thing. I didn't refute the title; I was living a fantasy.

One day I decided to drop by Dia's summer job at the University of South Alabama to surprise her with flowers and balloons. That was the way my dad raised me. Even though I was violating some of his principles of honesty and integrity by seeing three different women, my first thought was always to do something nice for others. Not many guys my age did anything extra for women.

As I carried the gifts into the office building on campus where Dia worked, I was shocked to see Vernie, one of the other women I was talking to, sitting at the front reception desk. She looked just as surprised as I did! In all our conversations, I never thought to ask where she worked. It never crossed my mind that she may have known Dia, let alone work in the same office with her.

The moment was awkward to say the least.

"Are those for me?" Vernie asked, referring to the flowers and balloons.

"No, they're not," I said, breaking the bad news to her. I took a deep breath and braced for her reaction. The expression on her face immediately went from joyful to bitter.

"Well, who are you here to see then?" she asked in a salty tone.

Feeling worse by the minute, I said, "I'm here to see Dia…"

"Dia Evans?" she blurted out, cutting me off. "Why are you bringing flowers for Dia? Are you talking to her?"

I didn't have to respond. Standing there holding flowers and balloons that were for Dia and not for her was answer enough. Vernie was clearly pissed.

"You wait here," she seethed. "I'll go confer with the manager, and we'll see if Dia can see you." I could sense that asking the manager was a form of retaliation from Vernie, but all I could do was wait.

Vernie took her time asking the manager. When she returned, I sat across from her, waiting in the chair. I could tell she was fuming on the inside. Even though our friendship had never extended beyond flirting, I understood why the situation made her feel upset; I felt guilty. I figured I would apologize later when the timing was better. She was in no mood to hear "I'm sorry" at that moment, so I sat there quietly.

After waiting for about ten minutes, Dia and her manager came out of the back. I stood up, holding a bouquet of flowers and balloons for Dia. That's when the unthinkable happened. The manager who walked out with Dia was Eva, the third woman I was talking to! I almost dropped the flowers on the floor. Not only did Vernie work with Dia, but Eva did too. She was the manager for both of them.

Eva also assumed the flowers and balloons were for her. At that point, I was completely sunk. My initial instinct was to run out of the office. Instead, I began stuttering through another explanation that I was there to see Dia. That's when I handed Dia the flowers and balloons. As I did so, Vernie and Eva both put it together that I was talking to all of them.

Moments later, all three of them started chewing me out. None of my explanations were making sense or helping. Vernie and Eva were hurt; they felt like I had betrayed them. Even Dia was angry. She knew I was seeing other women, but she didn't know that they were Vernie and Eva, her coworker and her boss, and neither did I.

I had no other options at that point. I managed a weak apology.

"I'm sorry, y'all." I turned and walked out.

After that, none of them returned my phone calls. I was disappointed in myself for not being more respectful and transparent with the three of them. I also resented Chris for giving me the stupid label of "Playa from the Himalayas." That's when I realized I should have been strong enough to resist peer pressure and stay true to who I was. I couldn't really be mad at anyone but myself for growing overconfident by the thought that I had arrived. I'd never play the Playa role again! It wasn't who I was. I realized the extent to which I had lost myself. My boundaries were blurred by my success, and I had overreached in ways my dad had always warned me against, overlooking my values along the way. #lostfocus, #beyourself, #notaplaya, #resistpeerpressure, #upholdvalues

☼ **Words of Wisdom** ☼
"There is a thin line between being a victor and being a villain. That line is called integrity and it doesn't take much to fall off."
–John Stallworth, Sr.

BLOOMING WHERE
PLANTED

Seeds of Leadership

After getting settled working at the manufacturing plant, I started thinking of ways to improve. Although I was making a good salary for someone my age and had lots of opportunities to earn additional income by working overtime, my primary focus was to become a more valuable employee for the company. By improving my personal skills, I would be a better employee and, in turn, reap more opportunities for growth. I routinely volunteered for additional tasks at work, and I explored the option of going to college. To my surprise, I learned that many manufacturing facilities avoid hiring workers with college degrees to do shift work and manual labor in plants and factories. Generally, degreed workers have greater options to progress professionally and are viewed as overqualified for shift-work positions. It's not unusual for companies to reserve a large number of plant-based roles, including in management, for non-degreed workers to aspire to and fill. This creates a path for non-degreed workers with high aspirations to achieve promotions beyond working on the factory floor. Jobs like shift supervisor, production supervisor, and area supervisor may be reserved for employees without college degrees. In the absence of having a degree, they were influential plant-based roles I would have opportunities to earn in the future.

We periodically had corporate executives for the company come to speak to employees about future business and how plant operators have a big impact on the overall success of the company. Most employees didn't pay much attention to these executives. Those workers felt they were just blowing smoke. However, I was always interested in learning a little more about the company. I genuinely wanted to do more to help the company be successful. Some of the executives spoke in terms that were too complex for me and other plant employees to grasp. In the process, many of us were lost in the first two or three minutes of their presentations. Without realizing their disconnection from their audience, some of these executives would ramble on for 30 to 40 minutes, making speeches that essentially meant nothing to most of the plant population. But that was their view of leadership engagement. They thought it was a good way of getting employees on board with their ideas. Thinking of my dad's view of being rich and poor, these corporate executives were in poverty and didn't know it. Even though they earned hundreds of thousands of dollars a year, they were poor in their ability to communicate and to connect. It was a valuable lesson for me to know and understand my audience.

One of the executives, Carlo Canela, was very unusual in his approach. He customized and crafted his messaging in simple enough terms that even I could understand. Not only did Carlo have passion and a clear vision for what he wanted to do with his segment of the business, he was also able to really communicate the messaging for plant operators. I was mesmerized as he spoke. After a couple of his visits to the plant, I made sure I wouldn't miss his presentations. Carlo was truly wealthy in his ability to reach any audience, to articulate messaging, and to get people to follow him by building trust. His true wealth didn't involve his financial status or job role in the company.

As non-degreed operators at the plant, we had rules for communicating with corporate executives. We were instructed to never send direct communications to an executive without first having it approved by the site management team. This directive mostly existed to make sure messaging was consistent and ensure plant leaders would not be caught off guard by anything unexpected. However, Carlo's ability to connect with others gave me enough confidence to overcome my fear of approaching him. At the end of one of Carlo's speeches, I decided to walk up to him and tell him I appreciated his presentations. I was extremely nervous, but I told him his messaging really meant a lot to me as an operator, and that it encouraged me to work harder. To my surprise, Carlo asked me to send him an email to stay in touch. This was an unusual request for a corporate executive to make from a plant operator. Without Carlo's gift of connection, my shyness and lack of confidence would have won out, and I would have missed this great opportunity. Carlo was definitely a Gem Seeker.

Once I got back to the plant control room from his town hall meeting, I reflected further on Carlo's message, which was about empowering us all to embrace our differences, especially the floor workers. He felt we had a lot of potential, but we didn't realize it. He wanted us to know that we played an integral role in the success of the company. His message was similar to my dad's. We all have gifts. Regardless of our position at the plant, we all had the power to be successful and to prosper. Carlo's message was especially important to me at that point in my career. I wanted to do more but didn't know how. There were rules, some unwritten, at the plant that I felt were restrictive. I had to make a strategic decision to either follow the unwritten rules or take a calculated risk which might open more doors for me to grow.

On the control room computer, I quickly started working on a thank-you email to Carlo. I rushed to compose the email because another executive had made a comment previously that had stuck with me. "Always reply to communication within 24 hours," the other executive had said. "It gives others a great feeling when you respond quickly. If you show respect, people will give more respect in return." It was a simple but powerful message that resonated with me because it was in line with my perspective of reaping what you sow in the form of giving respect to others. It would ultimately lead to my gain. Working on the email to Carlo, my hands were shaking to a point that I could barely type. I must have read and reread the message a hundred times before I felt like it was good enough to send.

The company rules were very clear about notifying local management before sending a message to corporate executives. I intended to send Carlo the message without copying anyone, even though it was a no-no. I hoped Carlo and I had developed a good enough rapport for me to send him a direct message. For this simple thank-you email, I was willing to take the risk.

Later that night on the night shift, after reading my short paragraph a dozen more times, I felt ready to send the email to Carlo. A huge sense of anxiety engulfed me. The email could get me blackballed for the rest of my time with the company, preventing me from gaining promotions and leaving me without options to advance from the plant floor for the rest of my career. I tried not to think about the negative implications of sending it. After much deliberation, I hit the "Send" button.

I immediately had self-doubt about whether or not I had done the right thing. I wasn't well versed in wording messages or communicating with people outside of my direct sphere of association. I didn't really know Carlo, yet I had the audacity to communicate with him directly at the risk of losing my job or my opportunities to grow in the company. What would Carlo think of me? I nervously went back to my job on the plant floor, filling up the drums with our product, feeling vulnerable and exposed as I worried about the email. It was a long hour on the packaging line.

By the time I made it back to the control room from the packaging line, I looked at my email and couldn't believe my eyes. Carlo had replied to my message within ten minutes of me sending the email. It was after midnight, but he said he wanted to reply to me before going to bed. He wrote that our conversation after the meeting had meant a lot to him. He said he had spoken at 20-plus manufacturing sites, and I was the first operator to confirm that his messaging was actually reaching the plant floor.

Just that quickly, his words eased my fears and anxieties about sending the email. I felt a tremendous relief to learn that my email wasn't negatively perceived. My simple words of gratitude made a big difference to him. I was happy to know that nothing I said in the email offended him, but more so I felt a sense of worth and value I couldn't explain. That little confidence made me feel rich internally. Carlo and I kept in touch without anyone knowing.

During the next town hall meeting, Carlo was very particular to mention having great communications with the operations team. At the same time, he told the entire plant it was important for people to have open dialogue without any restrictions. He wanted plant employees to email or call him directly without involving others. His support was a game-changer. He encouraged me without naming me publicly, and he also opened the lines of communication so that anyone could email him at any time. This gesture made it acceptable for me to continue messaging him without fear of retaliation for communicating with him directly.

In some instances, company executives don't consider the many barriers their employees are facing. A critical part of being an effective leader is helping employees break down walls to take advantage of their diverse ways of thinking. #takeachance, #knowyouraudience, #bedifferent, #overcomeselfdoubt, #gamechanger

Above and Beyond

I began looking for more ways to make improvements in the processes around me. I was fortunate to work with the local IT manager, Barbara Brunson, on several improvement projects that taught me how to use Microsoft Access, Excel, Word, and

Micrografx FlowCharter. These skills allowed me to convert over 1900 rarely accessed paper manuals into electronic format that plant workers could easily use on computers. I created a database called the "Mobile Process Support System" (MPSS) that is still in use today. That application enabled us to convert hundreds of handwritten work instructions and manuals into an electronic format that was easily accessible. This significantly reduced the time it took to train new operators and increased product consistency. It was a monumental undertaking that I did in my off time.

The extra work did not go unnoticed. My efforts caught the eye of one of the senior plant leaders, and he decided to give me more opportunities to improve other areas of the plant, such as helping make end-of-shift reports available digitally. The additional work significantly improved my skills and led to an invitation to work on a corporation-wide manufacturing improvement team. This opportunity would allow me to visit various locations for knowledge sharing and collaboration with other departments. After successfully working on several small improvement projects at the plant, I definitely wanted to do more. However, I didn't believe I had the ability to impact change in a way that some of the engineers would, so I knew pursuing a degree in engineering was the right path for me.

Face Time with the CEO

I was soon invited to Chicago for a meeting. We assembled at the Royal Melbourne Country Club, an exclusive venue for our team meeting. From what I understood, Michael Jordan was a member of the country club. It was a beautiful place with a well-manicured golf course. I was one of the first ones to arrive at the event. While walking around the building admiring the architecture and marveling at the fact that I was actually there, I walked around the corner and bumped into Mitch Wingate, president and CEO of the company. He was full of energy and especially talkative. I couldn't believe my good fortune when he invited me to stroll along with him. As we walked around the clubhouse making small talk, Mitch said he couldn't believe the amount of wealth the country club members had. He said that many of the elaborate mansions surrounding the golf courses were actually owned by young people. His comments echoed one of the lessons I had learned from my dad, who would say, "Often those who seem rich are in debt over their heads and dirt poor. It's a tough way to live, but it's the path of many."

After about 30 minutes of talking with Mitch, I started feeling uncomfortable that I was consuming too much of his time. Mitch insisted it was fine. He continued talking with me until most of the visitors arrived. It was a great conversation in many ways. He even asked what I wanted to do in life. I told him I wanted to make a difference. I told him I had started college at the University of South Alabama to get a chemical engineering degree and that it was extremely difficult. He was shocked that I was actually doing it while working shift work. More than anything, this experience showed me that with just a dash of confidence, I could hold my own in a conversation with the president and CEO of a large corporation.

🪨 Cracks in The Wall 🪨
Hidden Gems, don't be afraid to talk to people in power. Gem Seekers, be accessible. Relish in the opportunity to engage, and view helping others as a wealth-building practice. **These moments of connection breach the wall and bring us together.**

The manufacturing improvement team group members and I clumsily mingled around the Royal Melbourne's clubhouse. We were clearly visiting for the first time and out of our element as we admired the lush scenery and enjoyed the delicious food. This particular gathering was more of a casual get-together and not a formal discussion or presentation by the leaders. I ran into several corporate executives during that event, including Carlo Canela. Carlo and I spoke just briefly before Mitch Wingate took to the stage to give the welcoming speech. Mitch spoke for only a few minutes. Toward the end of his speech, he said "I want to say one thing about one of the people here. His name is Ronnie Stallworth. Ronnie, come up to the front of the room if you don't mind."

I was terrified as I wove through the crowd filled with people from all parts of the world and made my way to the front of the large ballroom. Mitch put his arm around my shoulder and said, "You see this guy? He is an operator at our manufacturing plant in Mobile, Alabama. We spent about an hour talking today. He's working shift work and going to school to get his chemical engineering degree. Keep an eye on him because he is going to do something special with his life when he finishes. I can't wait to see what he does for this company." Then everyone cheered as I stood there stunned! There I was, gaining recognition for being a humble person who was passionate about improving the work environment without expecting anything in return. It was a great experience. While his words of encouragement caught me off guard, they also motivated me to keep trying my best in school.

Mitch Wingate then arranged for me to go to a Chicago Cubs baseball game at Wrigley Field during that same trip. I had great tickets, sitting on the third-base line directly behind the dugout—the best seats in the house. As I sat there, I was extremely grateful for the opportunity. I was a poor kid from Mobile Terrace sitting at Wrigley Field, eating a hotdog, drinking a beer, and listening to Harry Caray sing 'Take Me Out to the Ball Game' with Sammy Sosa warming up on deck. You couldn't tell me I wasn't blessed with wealth! That experience was confirmation for me that I could gain internal wealth by just being myself and not dwelling solely on my finances. The calculated risks I took in reaching out to these executives paid off with great returns.

🔹 Cracks in The Wall 🔹

There are always inherent risks associated with investments. But few risks have a greater return on investment than developing yourself as a Hidden Gem, or developing someone else as a Gem Seeker, to make the greatest difference possible in the world. **It's worth the risk to invest in opportunities to make positive change.** *Taking these chances will rarely be easy, no matter which side of the wall you're on.*

My connection with Carlo Canela and the trip to Chicago where I met Mitch Wingate, were, again, life-changing experiences for me. After spending an appreciable amount of time with Carlo, Mitch, and the administrative assistants from the executive leadership team, I was in a perpetual state of awe. From the moment I was picked up in a limousine from Chicago O'Hare Airport, the level of detail the administrative team had put into every single element made sure my experience was memorable. The exposure was yet another data point for me to gain firsthand knowledge of how executive leaders should treat people and also how other people lived. It was a different level of what good looks like. I could barely contain my excitement of someday being able to take my kids to a Chicago Cubs baseball game and letting them walk through beautiful homes like the ones I had marveled at from the grounds of the Royal Melbourne Country Club. I had never experienced anything like it growing up in Mobile. There was something magical about traveling to other cities and witnessing these things firsthand! It made them tangible for me, and I yearned to experience more of them.

Carlo and Mitch were excellent corporate executives who clearly cared about their employees. They proved that executives could be nice, caring, and also effective leaders. The company flourished under their leadership. Earlier in my career, I had experienced what good looked like on a smaller scale when I was at Nation Automotive with my two store managers and the general manager. Their leadership styles gave me a fundamental sense of how I wanted to be as a leader, even though it was at a single store and not an entire organization. Once I reached the manufacturing plant, several local leaders cemented my foundational thinking about great leadership. It started with Jack Gardner. In his role as the HR manager for the plant in Mobile, he was in an excellent position to be a Gem Seeker. He gave me countless opportunities to show my value at the plant and constantly encouraged me to go to school. He was an advocate for my continued growth and development when I faced push-back from others who couldn't or didn't want to see my potential. He was influential and strategic in how he submitted my name for certain roles, and he actively searched for other plant floor workers who also had the ability to take on more responsibilities.

Another leader at the plant was Tim Early. Tim was an engineer, one of the smartest people I had ever been around, and he had the unique ability to make things simple. Most of the other engineers were focused on themselves, trying to show the plant floor employees how smart they were. They thought it gave them power to use complex words and equations and talk over our heads. Tim was just the opposite. He would take extra time to help the entire team, including the plant floor employees, understand the path forward and why things were done a certain way. Ultimately it allowed his entire department to routinely excel above the other departments. Tim was consistently courted by executive leadership to take on corporate-level roles, but that wasn't his desire. He loved working in the plant setting, mentoring people like me and spending quality time with his family. In my dad's earlier example about the comparison between wealthy and poor people, Tim was wealthy beyond belief, and he was living life the way most humble and grateful people dream of. He freely shared his wealth of knowledge with everyone he met. These leaders set the standard for how I intended to live my life! #stepchange, #betterlifeforkids, #getdatapoints, #pacesetter, #trueleadership

Crabs in a Bucket

To bring reality back to the positive and optimistic experiences I had with successful leaders, I also had the experience of dealing with supervisors who prolonged my struggles and, for many of my colleagues, completely suppressed their will to progress. I call these types of supervisors "pseudo-leaders." These are people that are imposters. Recognizing pseudo-leaders is extremely important because they cause more harm than good and are often in roles for some reason other than having the ability to actually do them. They undermine the character of good people, slowly bring down the morale in their sphere of control, and actively attempt to stifle the growth of anyone they perceive as a threat. It's important for Hidden Gems and Gem Seekers to recognize pseudo-leaders. Hidden Gems should beware of them, and influential Gem Seekers should weed them out of the system. Five key traits of a pseudo-leader include the following:

1. They are unhappy when others get attention, promotions, or positive recognition.
2. They go out of their way to block the success of others, even if it puts them in a bad light.
3. They don't realize that by helping others, they create more opportunities for themselves.
4. They have an entitlement mindset of wanting something without earning it.
5. They have a strong affinity for negative events and are fueled by gossip, backbiting, and seeing things go wrong.

In a roundabout way, my dad warned me about pseudo-leaders when I was a kid growing up along the Gulf of Mexico. His lesson was given during one of our favorite pastimes, crabbing in Mobile Bay. He would get us up early in the morning and take us near the USS Alabama battleship where we'd go underneath the overpass and collect crabs. He used the crabs in his gumbo mostly, but we also had crab boils. He'd add Conecuh sausage, corn, and a few shrimp to the mix, and we'd sit around a fire pit eating them until late at night. The trips were fun for us because not only were we catching delicious blue crabs, but we were also spending quality time with my dad during the day. We'd be there for hours talking about some of his stories and adventures growing up while we periodically checked the baskets to see if another crab had found the chicken backs that we used as bait.

As we prepared for one of our trips, I noticed Dad taking only a five-gallon bucket to hold the crabs. He never worried about bringing a lid for the bucket. When I asked, he said we didn't need a lid. I was afraid the crabs would crawl out of the bucket and hop back in the water to freedom or, even worse, pinch one of us!

As the morning progressed, we'd catch one or two crabs every five to ten minutes. Soon the bucket started filling up. The more crab we caught, the more nervous I grew, worrying about them escaping. I wasn't convinced that we didn't need a lid on the bucket. After dropping each crab in the bucket, I'd look at my dad to see if he still thought we were okay. He would simply shrug his shoulders and brush off my concern, reassuring me that I didn't need to worry because they wouldn't get out.

I watched the bucket continue to fill up until it was about two-thirds full. Just as my dad had assured me, we hadn't lost a single crab. I was certain that was about to change. As I watched, I noticed that each time we added a new crab, it would scramble to get out of the bucket. Then other crabs would latch onto its leg and claws and pull it back down into the bucket. It was interesting to watch them pull each other back into the bucket versus working together to escape, like in the image below. They represented the pseudo-leaders that I would experience at the manufacturing plant. I was surprised because I had seen the opposite behavior from ants. When ants need to climb out of a hole or cross a barrier, they connect to each other to essentially create a chain or bridge that other ants crawl over to reach their destination. Afterwards, the worker ants systematically attach to the other side to pull the remaining workers to safety. Working together

as a team, ants accomplish seemingly impossible feats. But not crabs. The crabs would never work together to escape the open bucket. After a while, they would simply stop trying. The fate of the entire bucket was sealed, and all the crabs were destined to perish in Dad's gumbo or crab boil.

As I grew older, my dad and I had many conversations about the behavior of the crabs in the bucket. He said only a handful of crabs had ever escaped the bucket and made it back to safety in the water. It was so rare that he never brought a lid crabbing, and he would always have a full bucket of crabs going home from each trip. He likened the behavior of the crabs to people that weren't used to having anything, like many pseudo-leaders. Yet if they'd simply work together, many more people would experience freedom.

When some of my coworkers learned that I was going to college, several immediately turned on me. Their actions reminded me of those crabbing trips with Dad. He taught me that some people are intimidated by a person who wants to improve. He told me that those same people can be like crabs in a bucket. If you try to climb out of the bucket, they will do everything they can to pull you back in because they are intimidated. Some of these people even feel like they are owed something; they are debilitated by a sense of entitlement. #pseudoleaders, #crabsinbucket, #entitlementmentality, #getoutofthebucket, #belikeants, #slowbutsteady

DEGREE OF PERSEVERANCE

Academic Agony

Making the decision to get a college degree was very difficult. I had struggled throughout school, mostly with reading and math. Reading at a slower pace and trying to understand the mathematical concepts was so time-consuming that it negatively impacted my other classes and crippled my overall learning trajectory. A key failure of mine prior to high school was not studying before class or before a test. In fact, I rarely knew when tests or assignments were due. With that mindset, I was in no position to actively participate in classroom discussions or to perform well on pop quizzes or tests. Furthermore, I would have no idea what homework to do when I got home, in the remote chance that I attempted to do work after school. I didn't experience significant change until I learned to start preparing ahead of time, which I didn't fully embrace until after high school.

Once I got out of high school and started working full time, I realized I still wanted to learn. I had already realized I would need a college degree to have access to the types of job roles that I admired the most. As if I were begging for punishment, I chose one of the toughest degrees to pursue—chemical engineering. Chemical engineering was difficult for even the brightest students who had built a strong science and mathematics foundation throughout their high school years. Then there was me—a student who barely made it through middle school and struggled through high school with very little math and science background. I enrolled at the University of South Alabama without really thinking about what I was getting myself into. I knew so little about college that one of the professors, Dr. Huddleman, had to give me step-by-step directions to find the administration building on the University of South Alabama's massive campus. He physically walked me over to sign up for the chemical engineering program and became my academic advisor. Completing the degree would be a daunting task. The original plan was to take six years to complete my Bachelor of Science degree in chemical engineering, since I could not go full time. In hindsight, it was a good thing I didn't know how far this projection was off—in the end, it took me thirteen and a half years to graduate from the University of South Alabama. Had I known that up front, I probably would have never attempted it.

After I eagerly jumped into college, I immediately hit my first real wall. I didn't know anything about calculus or chemistry. The professors were literally speaking another language. Nothing, and I do mean absolutely nothing, they said made any sense to me. Engineering students should have taken prep courses in high school. I had taken only basic math and one algebra class. After hitting this wall, my professor gave me a mathematics placement test and quickly determined that I needed to take essentially every foundational class between basic math and Calculus 1. I accepted the challenge. I didn't fully grasp what that meant with regard to the timeline for completing my degree; all those prerequisite courses would translate into additional years in school. All I knew was that I would have to take a lot of classes that would eventually lead to me getting my chemical engineering degree. I started with basic high-school algebra. I worked through the foundations of math, taking one or two classes here and there over the course of three years. By then, I had projected I would be halfway done with my degree. In reality, I hadn't even started earning any credit toward my major.

Work and school were not the only things in my purview. I started dating one of my classmates, Gina. She had a part-time job as a graphic designer and was very knowledgeable of computers. Our math and computer courses were complementary, so our dating was also valuable study time for both of us. The long study hours together quickly evolved from dating into us getting married. The combination of school, work, and my thirst to spend more time with Gina was taking a toll on me. I was taking one foundational class after another without taking any engineering classes to make me feel like I was getting closer to a degree. I decided to drop out of school.

After sitting out a year, I spoke with my HR manager, Jack Gardner. He and his wife, Olivia, had taught me so many things over the years. After Jack and I talked about my struggles, he talked me into re-enrolling in school. I stayed enrolled for another year, but I still couldn't take engineering classes because I hadn't completed the prerequisite courses. I dropped out again at the end of the year.

At that point I thought I was done with school. But during a visit to the barbershop, my barber told me how proud he was of me. He had watched me study in his barbershop waiting for my turn to get a haircut. His words of encouragement convinced me to enroll again. He told me to focus on just the one step in front of me. I needed to trust my advisor and not allow myself to get overwhelmed. The motivation from my barber fueled me for another year before I dropped out again. I concluded that my college career was over.

Then Jack Gardner gave me an ultimatum.

"You get your ass back in school. You have potential. If you want to have a successful future, you've got to get your degree," he demanded. It was enough—I enrolled again and completed a few more foundational classes.

A little over a year later, I dropped out again. I was mentally and physically exhausted from school. I had a checklist of the 48 curriculum classes required to earn my degree hanging on my wall. After five years, I had checked off only two of those classes. The rest of the classes I had taken were all foundational classes. When I dropped out this time, I spoke to Dr. Huddleman about my progress. He encouraged me to continue because I was getting close to finally taking some classes that would count toward my degree. We sat in his office for hours trying to figure out a schedule with the correct mix and match that would allow me to work my full-time shift job and still satisfy my course prerequisites. Dr. Huddleman was a fantastic advisor and Gem Seeker. I needed his patience and encouragement to help me get back on track.

Most of my colleagues were rooting for me to be successful. One of them, Brad Hamic, was determined to help me succeed. Brad would catch all kinds of flak from swapping shifts with me. He'd work my day shifts so I could go to class, and I'd work his nights. It was a really good arrangement that allowed me to make up ground on some of my missed classes. Some of the other guys would deliberately decline to work overtime that they'd normally work just to force me to work extra shifts. Brad would always come to the rescue and work my overtime. He played an integral part in me getting through several tough years midway through the curriculum.

C's Earn Degrees

In my sixth year at University of South Alabama (USA), I finally started taking a couple of classes that counted toward my engineering degree. I re-enrolled in the Calculus 1 class I had dropped out of five years earlier when I realized I wasn't ready for that advanced level of math. It was extremely difficult because my time between courses spanned several years. Due to the gap between learning the information in the foundational classes and finally applying it in my curriculum coursework years later, I had forgotten some of the material.

Life was the perfect storm. Overtime was high at work. I was working 60-72 hours a week on 12-hour shifts. I'd get off work at 7:00 AM and by the time I made it to school, I was falling asleep in class. When I was awake, my sleep-deprived brain could not absorb the information that I hadn't looked at in years. My situation required me to spend a great deal of additional time studying outside of class. One of my engineering professors, Dr. Asher, was very tough! I was in his Equilibrium Stages class, and he was unforgiving. USA had switched from a quarter system to a semester system. One of the reasons Dr. Asher's class was so difficult was that he gave only two tests per semester. The course was scheduled only once per year and was a prerequisite for all subsequent engineering classes. If I failed one of Dr. Asher's tests, I was doomed. Failure would automatically add an additional year to my time in school.

Dr. Asher was a notoriously brutal grader. One of my classmates had already flunked out of this class twice. His third time around, he failed again. It was the first time I had ever seen a student earn a zero on a test when he had pages of calculations and formulas that were at least partially correct. After his third failure, that student decided to transfer to a different school. I didn't want to fail; I simply had to figure out a way to prevail.

To help prepare for the class, I put a lot of time into learning calculations and the required formulas. My calculator was completely set up. I had programmed 70 percent of the required calculations into the calculator. I was in good shape going into the first test. Dr. Asher allowed us to use our calculators as much as we wanted. To my surprise, many of the questions were relatively easy. I quickly plugged the numbers into the formulas I had stored in my calculator, and it spit out the results. I was ahead of schedule on the test, and I had additional time to look over some of the questions a second time. As Dr. Asher called for us to turn in our papers, I felt great submitting the test.

The following Monday when we got back in class, Dr. Asher wrote the test statistics on the board in front of the class. The average score was 24 out of 100. My heart sank! How could such a smart group of students only get 24 percent of the questions correct? An audible gasp rippled across the classroom. We had five of the smartest students in the entire school in that class. If they made A's, then, by default, the rest of us were below 24 percent. We knew he was a brutal grader, but even for Dr. Asher, this was a super low class average. When I got my test back, I had a 31 out of 100. Since I didn't know professors scaled the grades based on the class average, my heart pounded, my forehead started sweating, and my eyes filled with tears. I immediately thought there was absolutely no way for me to recover and I'd end up sitting out another year of school until the course was offered again.

I spoke with Dr. Asher, and, to my surprise, he congratulated me on doing well on the test. He said my 31 would correspond to the grade of a low B! I could hardly believe it, but I was still disappointed because I had actually gotten all of the answers correct on my test. He said he couldn't give me any additional credit because I didn't show enough of my work. I showed him the formulas that I had in my calculator and how I had correctly used them on the test. It made no difference to him; he wouldn't change my grade.

Passing Dr. Asher's first exam was great, but I couldn't relax because I had to prepare to pass the second exam, which was even more important. A low B grade provided very little cushion for passing the final exam. I consumed most of my accrued work vacation studying for Dr. Asher's final exam and the Calculus 1 class. By the grace of God, I passed the Calculus 1 class with a C, and the Equilibrium Stages class with a B. I survived Dr. Asher. Phew!

After submitting my educational reimbursement papers for approval, one of the leaders at the manufacturing plant, Earl

Cullman, called me into his office to discuss the C that I made in calculus. He said, "Ronnie, a C may get you a reimbursement from the company. But in my eyes, it's a failure. What use will I have for an engineer with such low grades?" He shook his head a little as he signed the reimbursement and handed it to me.

"Thank you for the reimbursement," I answered, taking the form in my hand. "About my grades, all I can say is that I'm not a traditional student. I have a family. And unlike other students in my classes, I'm also working a full-time job here," I said.

"That's no excuse," he replied quickly. "You're going to have to do better."

I said nothing else. I could see that in his eyes I was a failure. It was another moment of discouragement that I had to work through within myself. I had to give myself the credit that Earl Cullman wouldn't give me. Earning that C, that passing grade in Calculus 1, was extremely difficult. I was trying to remember a hundred complex details from each class while also working overtime so that I could provide for my wife and my young son Ronnie Jr.

My typical class day consisted of paying students a little cash to help me stay awake in class after working a 12-hour night shift. I would get only 30 minutes of sleep in my car in the parking lot before my Calculus 1 class started on Mondays, Wednesdays, and Fridays. Sleep deprivation had taken a toll on me, and my circadian rhythm was constantly out of sync. My decision-making skills also suffered. I was already under peak stress from my job while attempting to get a chemical engineering degree. But one thing is certain—poor people have a spirit inside of them that is specially tuned to overcoming challenges. We can take a beating and figure out ways to get back up. Regardless of what Earl thought, I was fine with my C in Calculus 1. The same C that represented mediocrity for Earl represented my ability to overcome adversity and find a way to succeed anyway. One C wouldn't keep me from my degree. #innerstrength, #momentumkillers, #csearndegrees

Hidden Gems must accept the fact that they are not on a level playing field. Circumstances are not equal, and we can't always gauge our progress or success by a typical measuring stick. Earl used a generic metric when he viewed my C in Calculus 1 as being below standard when, in fact, it was totally understandable and acceptable considering the degree of difficulty I had outside of class. If I had believed in his standard/typical measure of success rather than knowing what success looks like to me, I would have likely dropped out of school again.

◈ Hidden Gem Moment ◈

*Sometimes we have to see in ourselves what other people refuse to see. **That's why it's important to cultivate confidence.** Even when we are not fully aware of our own strengths, we can still draw on them when others see us as weak.*

Slowpoke

After being in college for almost eight years, I started hearing all kinds of discouraging comments. People at work were telling me I was stupid for spending so much time working on a degree at my age. In their minds, a degree only took four years to complete, so to them I must have been a real dummy if after eight years I was still nowhere near being done. They knew I was going to school only part time, had a wife and a son, and was working shift work. It was easy for them to poke fun at my super slow pace. One of the plant engineers at my job, Edward Ankerson, even pulled me aside to reinforce the negative comments from my other co-workers.

"Man, Ronnie! You're still in school?" he asked.

"Yes, I'm taking as many classes as I can take," I answered.

"If you take only one or two classes, you'll be in school forever. It's stupid to waste so much of your time trying to get a degree. You're going to be 40 years old before you graduate. What good can you do as a new 40-year-old engineer?" Edward prodded, adding sarcastic laughter to the insult.

"Edward, if God blesses me to reach that age, I'd rather be 40 years old with a degree than without a degree," I said.

However, shortly after that exchange with Edward, I dropped out of school again. I was tired from the heavy overtime and deflated by the teasing at work, and I elected to leave school rather than continue dealing with the negativity toward me. To make matters worse, I felt guilty about the lack of time I was spending with my family, and I needed the break to get more of a work-life balance and stress relief. My wife, Gina, and I had our share of disagreements around the amount of time I spent in and out of school, the lack of budgeting that wreaked havoc on our finances, and the priorities for how we'd spend the few hours of our day together. The path forward was rarely clear around anything other than our care for Ronnie Jr. We had made a strategic decision when Ronnie Jr. was about two years old for Gina to pursue her master's degree. It was at a time when I was burned out on school, and the decision allowed her to pursue her aspirations. I was able to strategically work overtime in ways that minimally impacted Ronnie Jr. (e.g., from midnight to 4:00 AM) and develop a budget to improve our financial situation. The decisions made sense for the family at that time.

We all made sacrifices as a result of Gina and me being in and out of school and working long hours. However, we were very fortunate to have unwavering support from family members and friends to help with Ronnie Jr. His grandparents and other extended family members created a support system that allowed both Gina and me to make incremental progress toward a more stable future. While it wasn't always an ideal situation, we viewed it as a necessary commitment that would ultimately put us in a better situation, and eventually it did. As a family, Gina and I worked together to make sure Ronnie Jr. felt loved at every turn.

But it didn't take long before the break from school started to take a toll on me. I loved school and missed the learning environment. I had come so far and felt a drive to get it done. We had established a family budget, and my additional overtime had relieved some of the financial stresses in our household. I went to meet with my advisor, Dr. Huddleman, after work one day to check the status of my degree. He told me that the chemical engineering curriculum had changed during my absence and two additional courses were needed. It was disheartening to hear about another obstacle in what had already been a nearly insurmountable journey. To continue, I would need to immediately take Calculus 2 as a prerequisite for the next level of engineering courses. Unfortunately, I had taken Calculus 1 nearly two years earlier and had forgotten a significant amount of the content. I knew the gap in time would compound the degree of difficulty in passing the course, but after discussing it with Gina, I made the decision to re-enroll.

While struggling through the rigorous trials at school, Curtis Barnes, my area supervisor at the manufacturing plant, was going out of his way to block me from continuing my education. He even threatened to not sign my educational reimbursement form, even though the company supported students going to college by paying 80% of the cost. His authority as my supervisor posed a dilemma. Whenever I pressed the issue about him signing my reimbursement form, I would suddenly get called in to work more overtime. This caused me to miss classes. Curtis also told the shift foremen,

Syrus Melvin and Rich Brice, to keep a close check on me and discipline me if I showed any signs of decreased productivity at work or excessive sleepiness on night shift.

"If Ron falls asleep, write his ass up and send him home!" Curtis warned.

Syrus and Rich followed Curtis' strict instructions. Syrus took it a step further and shared what Curtis said with other plant operators on my shift. One of them, Oscar, routinely fell asleep on night shift. Oscar fell asleep right in front of Syrus while he was in the process of being deputized to keep an eye on me, but nothing happened to him. Curtis' instructions were to send only me home if I fell asleep. Curtis, Syrus, and Rich all had the "crabs in a bucket" mentality my dad had taught me about. They saw me trying to climb up and couldn't resist pulling me back down.

My dad said if you didn't have something good to say about someone, keep quiet. I did my best to do just that and uplift people whenever possible. In the case of Curtis and the people he deputized to do his dirty work, they fit the exception in my dad's qualifying statement. They were willfully causing harm to me or others by their actions, and I owed it to myself and others to step up and help rectify the situation in a positive and constructive manner. They were textbook pseudo-leaders and warranted getting called out for their actions to hopefully improve the lives of others going forward.
#whatgoodlookslike, #bewareofcrabs, #smallmindedpeople,

#naysayers, #worklifebalance, #focusonthefamily, #stoppseudoleaders

The next stretch of school was the toughest so far. Even after dropping out several times, I started to see that I could actually finish if I put my head down and ground out the last few courses in the curriculum. I had gotten a promotion at work, and my new job responsibilities at the manufacturing plant required me to take work home frequently as it was a 24-hour operation. Because I knew my area supervisor didn't support me going to college, I started back at school without asking for reimbursement. Unfortunately, this also meant paying for my classes out of pocket without getting reimbursed. I had completed nearly twelve years of school while working full time and supporting my family. I could see the light at the end of the tunnel, but it wasn't the end of the road for me. To make the remaining time in school more manageable, I transferred to a less-demanding position in our distribution warehouse. The shift was 3:00 PM to 11:00 PM, but the job didn't require me to take work home. I had finally reached my senior-level engineering coursework, which required additional study time outside of classes. I also needed and wanted to spend more quality time with my family.

The distribution warehouse job reduced my workload to a reasonable level. The new job role was also at an off-site distribution warehouse, away from the faster-paced 24/7 manufacturing plant. Ironically, two of my colleagues at the distribution warehouse were preachers. Both of them gave me continuous encouragement and prayed for me to endure. It took everything in my power to get through the courses and I thank God for putting these two preachers in my path. They were instrumental in keeping me motivated. #godshelpers, #beprepared, #prayersanswered, #barbershopadvice

I only had the last few senior engineering classes remaining. Even with the reduced workload, my family responsibilities and the rigorous senior design classes were still tough to juggle. Then, by some fortunate twist of fate, the company offered me an early retirement package. My company was going through a tough spell. They were offering severance packages that included 1.5 weeks of pay for every year of service. With my fifteen years of service, I qualified for nearly six months of pay and full insurance benefits. Early retirement was a no-brainer on paper because it would give me a chance to go to school full time. I took the severance package and was off to complete my degree. #fulltimestudent, #godstiming, #earlyretirement

My decision to take the severance package was a huge risk. Not only did I give up one of the most stable and well-paying jobs in the region, but it also put my entire family's well-being at risk. We had a young son, financial obligations, and some people at the local manufacturing plant viewed my decision negatively. But Albert Arlington, one of the company's corporate vice presidents, made my decision feel more reasonable during a conversation we had about my future plans.

Albert and I had met years earlier during my company trip to Chicago. He knew my work ethic and was confident that the company's outlook would improve, and, once I finished school, I'd be a great employee for rehire. He was a mentor and Gem Seeker and wanted to see me succeed. Gem Seekers must be willing to openly display their confidence and strategically take chances on Hidden Gems. Having Albert's vote of confidence that he would rehire me after I completed my degree help put me at ease about the decision. My family and I reworked our budget and cut our household expenses to make ends meet. By making major decisions as a family, we were all committing to a plan that we could live with.

A Simple Engineering Problem

If you aren't an engineer, it might be difficult to grasp the pressure engineering students are under when they are being graded. Many engineering exams don't have multiple-choice questions. They have complex word problems that require multiple calculations, formulas, and theories to arrive at solutions. For this reason, answers to exam questions often vary depending on assumptions that each student must make.

For example, consider this sample exam question—How much does tire pressure change if it's measured with the tire off of the vehicle as opposed to when it is on the vehicle and holding the weight of the car?

To solve this problem, students must make a number of assumptions. Each student taking this exam may make different assumptions. Some assumptions include the following:

- If the ambient temperature of the tire is **hot or cold** prior to loading it with the weight of the car
- If the tire is **thick enough** to prevent its tube from expanding in other directions during loading
- If the tire's rubber is **infinitely stretchy** and only the steel belts inside of it provide the strength (i.e., the tire may deform a bit where it touches the ground)
- If the tire is **filled with air** and not water (some tractor tires have water in them)
- If there is **no tube** in the tire

Depending on the student's assumptions, each answer to the question may be different. It is up to the professor to determine if an assumption is valid enough to give full, partial, or no credit to the student on the exam. Test scoring is somewhat subjective because correct answers are only part of the goal in engineering. Being right is relative on an engineering exam. It's just as important to understand the concepts, logic, and practicality of a solution and to make valid assumptions. A professor could give two students two different grades for the same exact answer based on his opinion of how the student arrived at the answer. Or based on other factors that aren't so fair. #multiplesolutions, #manyrightanswers

Dr. No

One more year. That's all I had left, and I'd be done. One year left, but it was the calm before the storm. Trouble was brewing ahead in my final classes. One of our regular professors, Dr. Draeger, had to take a leave of absence from his teaching position. As a substitute, he brought in one of his friends, Dr. Carrera, to teach his Senior Thermodynamics course. Dr. Carrera was really not qualified to teach the high-level engineering class. While he may have been competent in some respects, he didn't know how to grade our assumptions on Senior Thermodynamics exams. To help Dr. Carrera, Dr. Draeger provided him with guidance for assessing the students in his class. We had all been taking Dr. Draeger's classes since the beginning of the engineering program. From the beginning of the class, it appeared that Dr. Carrera was content with giving students the same grade they had received in previous classes with Dr. Draeger. Even if we had improved and performed better in the current class, it was easy for him to simply keep the status quo. In my case, since I had taken early retirement, I was no longer working 60-70 hours a week. The quality of my work was significantly better once I became a full-time student, and most of my current grades were A's. His approach put me at a disadvantage.

I noticed this was happening when I received my first test back from Dr. Carrera with a C on it. I had worked hard and thought I should have received an A. I quickly compared my results to those of Jacob Walton, one of my study partners. Jacob was, without a doubt, the smartest student in our entire engineering cohort. We had just studied a very similar question the night before in our study group.

"I thought I did well on this exam. Let's compare answers," I told Jacob.

To our surprise, we had the same answers. Jacob had an A on his test. I should have made an A as well. I stared in anger at my C and immediately wanted justice.

The next day, I carried my test and a copy of Jacob's test to Dr. Carrera during his office hours.

"Dr. Carrera, I'd like to talk to you about the grade I received on my test," I said from the doorway. I felt calm and confident that he was going to change my grade.

"Sure, come on in, let's discuss it," Dr. Carrera said.

I entered the office and showed him my exam paper. I didn't show him Jacob's right away. We started going through the first question step by step.

"Ok...ok...ok...," Dr. Carrera said to himself as we looked over my answers together. I felt even more confident.

"Yes, these are correct," Dr. Carrera confirmed.

"Well, you gave me only partial credit. Why?" I asked.

"I wanted you to show me more of your work," Dr. Carrera answered.

I pointed out the formulas I used and the assumptions I made to arrive at my answers, which were handwritten on the page.

"Are you going to change my grade?" I asked.

"No," Dr. Carrera answered.

"I went over the answers with Jacob Walton," I said, pulling the copy of Jacob's exam from my backpack to show him. "We studied together and worked on a very similar problem the night before the exam. I know how to work it."

I placed Jacob's test side by side with mine on Dr. Carrera's desk. It was clear that my exam had more detail and showed more steps for how I arrived at my answer when solving the problem. Dr. Carrera looked down at the two exams together with a brief glance.

"Yes, I see," he said, nodding his head in what seemed like agreement.

"So, now are you going to change my grade?" I asked, again.

"No." Dr. Carrera answered again.

"Give me a similar question and I'll work it here on the spot," I offered.

"The grade is final," he replied.

"Why won't you change my grade when you see now that I know how to work the problem?" I asked, surprised that he was ignoring my compelling evidence.

"I'm not going to change it because you didn't show enough detail," said Dr. Carrera.

"I showed more detail than Jacob," I replied.

"Well, Jacob doesn't need to show me the details because I know he knows how to work the problem," Dr. Carrera said.

"Let's look at the next problem, Dr. Carrera," I said.

"I don't need to look at it. I'm not changing the grade," said Dr. Carrera.

I could see Dr. Carrera had no willingness to compromise. I left his office. #insecureteacher, #preconceivednotions, #inflexibility

◆ Hidden Gem Moment ◆

Hidden Gems will almost always have to overcome being branded and labeled as inferior. They'll have to show more work to prove themselves. **They'll have to do more than others to break through barriers so people can see their true abilities.** *Hidden Gems must keep looking through these cracks and breaking through those openings so that people can see their capabilities. Eventually, the right people will see that Hidden Gems are able to achieve significantly more when given the opportunity.*

One and Done

Later, I filed a grievance with the department chairman. Little did I know this would come back to haunt me. I didn't realize it at the time, but Dr. Draeger, the regular professor who had taken a leave of absence and recommended Dr. Carrera to replace him, was the reviewer of the grievance. By filing the grievance, I had unknowingly made my final year in school exponentially more difficult. I still had to take one more course with Dr. Draeger—Senior Design, my very last course to graduate.

I had terrible anxiety going into my last semester of school. Even though I did pass Senior Thermodynamics with a C, I knew Dr. Draeger was going to hold a grudge against me for filing a grievance against his friend and hand-chosen substitute, Dr. Carrera. And Dr. Draeger was the only person standing between me and my degree. Senior Design was offered only once a year. Failing the class would mean sitting idle for an entire year until it was offered again, delaying the completion of my degree. By the start of the second semester of my final year, Dr. Draeger was back, and he was angry. We both knew that it was going to be a long last semester for me.

I started my Senior Design class with Dr. Draeger. In prior semesters, Dr. Draeger had allowed students to pick their own design teammates. This semester, Dr. Draeger assigned teammates. The composition of the design teams is a crucial factor for success in this final class. Teammates coordinate schedules and delegate project tasks aligned with each teammate's strengths, working together on every element of a complete design project.

As I expected, Dr. Draeger grouped me with two other students that had received poor feedback in the prior semester's Design class. He knew if I was going to pass his class, I'd have to complete almost all the work on my own. This was his way of expressing his displeasure about the grievance I had filed against his friend in his absence.

As the class progressed, things played out just as I feel Dr. Draeger intended. My two teammates had routine conflicts that prevented them from completing their portions of the project on time. This caused major problems, and I had no recourse but to do almost all the work on my own.

Our project was to design a complex three-phase separator. The project was broken up into three portions. The economics portion addressed the financial sustainability of the operation of the separator, ensuring that the design didn't cost more money than the value it brought. The hydraulics portion addressed the flow of material through the separator. The flow allows for the separation of solids, liquids, and gases, ensuring that contents from the separator could be salvaged. The metallurgy portion addressed the type of metal used to construct the separator. The separator must be designed in a way that its metals won't corrode prematurely during operation.

I had to learn and complete all three portions of the project to make sure it was successful. When the work was done, I simply informed my teammates of what I had done. For them, it was great because they didn't want to do the work anyway. We all had two other difficult courses to complete simultaneously, so they were happy to do the bare minimum for our Senior Design project throughout the entire semester.

We finally arrived at the last week of school and I had easily passed my other two courses for the semester. It was time to present our final three-phase separator design project, with all of the calculations and economics, as our final exam. Presentations were conducted in front of all students and several faculty members. It was a grueling day that lasted the better part of five hours. Our presentation was next to last to be presented. I believed Dr. Draeger designed the schedule that way intentionally, to give the reviewing professors a view of what "good" looked like before my team's presentation. One after another, design teams presented their final projects. The ones that were high quality had detailed calculations and interactive team participation that clearly demonstrated that all the teammates had contributed to the project.

The time arrived for my group to present our project as a team. As the three of us stood together in front of the class to present our assignment, my two teammates had no idea what was included in the content as they had done very little work on the project. I assumed they had at least looked over my work, which I had sent them periodically throughout the semester.

As I started describing my separator. I presented a very detailed slide deck, filled with graphics and calculations, projected on a large screen in the engineering lecture hall. I could see the look of surprise on Dr. Draeger's face, as well as the faces of Dr. Asher, Dr. Carrera, and Dr. Huddleman, who were all seated in the audience. Admittedly, I had certainly struggled through some of my earlier courses. But for this Senior Design class, I knew the details of my project inside and out, and it showed as I went through every intricate detail of my work. I had internalized the project so thoroughly that I was presenting without even looking at the screen.

After my presentation was over, many of the students watching were speechless, including my Senior Design teammates who hadn't worked on the project. I was confident that this was the best presentation of the semester by far. As Dr. Draeger and the other professors asked very difficult questions, I gave crisp and correct answers to them all, even for the portions of the project that were not assigned to me.

When the professors asked my teammates specific questions about their portions of the assignment, they had no clue how to respond because they hadn't done the work. Rather than let them struggle and risk failing the class, I answered the questions on their behalf. Soon, Dr. Draeger instructed me not to respond to any more questions. He wanted the other two students to answer, but neither one of them was able. It was apparent that I had done all the work for all three portions of the project. I was able to answer all questions, even the extremely random ones Drs. Draeger and Asher asked, hoping to throw me off my game.

That day it didn't matter. I was ready for them. I already had 15 years of solid manufacturing experience. I was even able to clarify a few academic assumptions that I knew wouldn't work in a real-world manufacturing site. They were so consumed with trying to stump me during the Q&A of my design presentation that the last group was nearly forgotten. It was hilarious.

The following Monday, I went to speak with Dr. Draeger about my grade. He complimented me on completing the entire design project and presentation. He also confirmed that he had paired me with the other two students on purpose.

"I wanted to make sure you understood the material," he said, handing me my final grade. "98 - Excellent Design Project!" was written on the front page of the grade sheet in big red letters.

I grabbed the paper out of his hand and drove home as quickly as I could to share the results with my family. After dropping out a dozen times and re-enrolling again over nearly 14 years, I finally graduated from the University of South Alabama with a BS in chemical engineering in 2003. I was the first in my immediate family to earn a degree. I was 36 years old, not 40 as Edward Ankerson had predicted. It was a long journey that was enabled by a lot of people taking a chance on me, making sacrifices to see me get through it.

The situation with Dr. Carrera had created another wall for me to breach. However, it was an anomaly at the University of South Alabama. All of my other experiences at the university were stellar! Even before I enrolled at South Alabama, residents in my neighborhood and other parts of the city were greatly influenced by the hope and excitement South Alabama generated through sports, the advanced medical facilities, and the impact on industry in the region. I remember going to a game at the Mobile Civic Center Arena as a kid to watch the USA Jaguars basketball team play, and I dreamed of playing for the Jags one day.

Another of my early exposures to USA was through my mom. She was an employee in the custodial department, which enabled me as a youth to use some of the facilities at no cost. I regularly played basketball in the recreation center while in high school. Once I enrolled as a student at USA, the level of support I received from the staff and professors, including Dr. Draeger, was outstanding. They freely provided hands-on guidance to navigate the engineering program, including multiple curriculum changes over the 14-year period, to make sure I didn't have any missteps that would have delayed my graduation date. As a nontraditional student, I received flexibility from the professors and department chair, where possible, on some assignments to accommodate my work and family commitments. At the same time, they didn't lower any standards or give me anything I didn't earn.

In addition to the coursework, the level of philanthropy from the alumni base was impressive. Their compassion for the school's continued growth was clearly evident by the constant erection of new buildings all over campus during my years there. I looked forward to becoming financially stable enough to give back to the university as a donor. Their generosity was one of the reasons I immediately started the Ron Stallworth Chemical Engineering Scholarship after graduating. Giving back to the university and community to help Hidden Gems like me was an honor that would have made my dad proud. I can credit the University of South Alabama for being the conduit that directly transitioned me from a Hidden Gem to a Gem Seeker. #leadbyexample, #gojags

A SEASON OF CHANGE
AND REFLECTION

Bound for the Windy City

By the time I graduated from USA in 2003, the economy had recovered and, as promised earlier, I received a call from Albert Arlington with a job offer. The position was based at the company's headquarters in Chicago. It was in the field technical services department and required approximately 75% travel domestically and internationally. Some assignments could last for months at a time. The job role was essentially a rite of passage to more lucrative salary opportunities in the future. There was a required commitment in the role of three years at minimum. Gina, Ronnie Jr., and I discussed the challenges of such a grueling travel schedule. We had all endured a lot by then and wanted to exhale a bit to enjoy the fruits of our labor. At the same time, we all agreed that taking the travel role would ultimately benefit us as a family in the future. One immediate perk was the paid family travel to anywhere I worked in the world. We'd all get to travel the globe and wouldn't have to pay a dime out of our pockets!

I accepted the job offer, and after spending the better part of a year traveling back and forth to the Middle East, Europe, and Asia, we learned that Gina was pregnant with our second son. It was exciting news, and the thought of Ronnie Jr. finally getting the baby brother he longed for was an added blessing. I was fortunate enough to be home for several months around the time of Jonathan's birth in early 2004. Seeing the excitement on Ronnie Jr.'s face was priceless, and I wanted to experience it with my family. The constant travel was mentally draining on all of us. On one hand, the road life, travel, and exposure created even more excitement than we had anticipated! At the same time, we all missed being together as a family. I knew it typically took about a year to transition off the road, so directly after Jonathan was born, I started searching for a job role with more stability. The final year on the road was tough but knowing there was a finite ending made it more manageable.

During one of my visits back home, Ronnie Jr. was nearly 10 years old, and Jonathan was almost one year old. We had gone several months without seeing each other and were forced to make the most of the three-days-home visit before I needed to travel to Singapore, on the island of Malaysia, for my next assignment. As the clock ticked closer to my departure time, I played with Ronnie Jr. and Jonathan as much as I could at Gina's parents' house in Alabama. We were all sad about me having to leave again.

When it was time for me to leave, I begrudgingly got into my car, and just as I was about to back out of the driveway, I saw Ronnie Jr. running out of the house waving for me to stop. I quickly hopped out of my car. With tears flowing down his face, he asked if he could ride on my back one more time before I left for the airport. He jumped on my back, and we ran around the yard with both of us crying every step of the way. With no more time to spare, I quickly dropped him at the door, and, with one last goodbye, I got back into my car and sped out of the driveway. We kept eye contact through the front window of the house for as long as we could until I was out of sight. It was one of the toughest trips I had ever taken. I cried the entire flight to Singapore and for the next week after arriving.

During my assignments, I missed my family and cried countless nights after calling home for our nightly routine to say prayers together before bedtime. When the pain of missing them became unbearable, my managers allowed me to take an extra trip back home to see them or have them visit me. Thank God I had excellent managers that were considerate of my situation. In the middle of the Singapore assignment, I was asked to help with an emergency assignment in Yeosu, South Korea. I had already been there several times and the refinery specifically requested me for the troubleshooting issue. I quickly shuffled schedules to travel from Singapore to Yeosu and made arrangements for my family to visit me there for a week. I had been gone for over a month and it was my first time seeing Jonathan walking. After completing the assignment, we took a few extra days to explore South Korea, including the historic Nagan Folk Village and the capital of Seoul. As a special blessing from God, it snowed on Christmas Eve for the first time in Yeosu in over 20 years, according to the locals. We made our first snowman together in the park across from the hotel. It was an experience of a lifetime for all of us!

After we all departed South Korea, I returned to Singapore to resume the assignment. I knew Singapore and Malaysia would be another great learning experience for my family, and since I had been flexible about taking on other tough assignments without complaining, my managers were happy to fly Gina and Ronnie Jr. to Singapore to spend nearly a month with me. Jonathan hadn't received all of his immunizations at the time, and we didn't want to risk taking him out of the US again for such a lengthy period. He stayed with Gina's parents during the trip. Having Gina and Ronnie Jr. in Malaysia with me was a wonderful experience that brought us all closer together! The separations were grueling, and Gina did a really good job of holding the pieces together, helping Ronnie Jr. and

Jonathan manage their emotions and carrying a tremendous load by herself during my lengthy assignments. After Gina and Ronnie Jr. departed Singapore, I knew it would be my last assignment before leaving that job role. We had all sacrificed enough!

Following the Singapore assignment, I took an office-based role at the company headquarters near Chicago. Just as we had planned, we had all reaped countless rewards from the two and a half years in the field technical services job role. Not only had my salary more than doubled, the experiences of traveling throughout different parts of Europe, Asia, and the Middle East was priceless.

My new office was located near Chicago, which required us to relocate from Alabama to the northwest Chicago suburbs in late 2005. The primary reasons for agreeing to the sacrifices over the years was to have the ability financially to expose Ronnie Jr. and Jonathan to a different lifestyle than I had growing up. While I wouldn't trade my childhood and poverty for anything, I wanted them to experience and learn from higher-level challenges and struggles, not basic needs such as no electricity, water, or television, or living paycheck-to-paycheck.

The move was a major step up for all of us. Even though I was technically based in Des Plaines, Illinois, near Chicago, I had spent the bulk of my time either on the road traveling or back in Mobile during my breaks between assignments. During one of my trips to Chicago, I was driving around looking for potential homes and spotted a nice, gated community with a golf course and large estate homes. It was Boulder Ridge Country Club in Lake in the Hills, Illinois, a suburb located about an hour and a half northwest of Chicago. After doing a little research, we found a perfect 5000 sq. ft. estate home in the neighborhood that was in a price range we could afford. It had a large backyard for the boys and us to enjoy and room for a small garden. Through our budgeting, we had put aside a sizable amount of cash for a down payment, and by consistently paying our bills on time, we qualified for a low-interest rate mortgage. We even added a custom movie theater in the basement. Being able to purchase that home was extremely gratifying! We had all learned tough lessons about sacrificing and overcoming challenges along the way. Our blessings were abundant!

The examples we set for Ronnie and Jonathan about working together for the best interest of the family were extremely beneficial for their development. They consistently saw us setting challenging personal goals with school and work, saving, and investing, paying our debts on time to build our credit, and saying "no" to things that were outside our budget. In doing so, we were able to reach much greater heights. All our lives had changed forever! #expandedfamily, #newbeginnings, #noplacelikehome, #familylove, #homesick, #thewindycity

The Jetsetters

The international travel and ventures into other cultures did wonders for our global perspectives. It made all of us thirsty for more, and we were open to explore job roles that allowed us to take a long-term international assignment all together as a family. My previous assignment in Singapore on the Malay peninsula had been a chance to do just that. It represented the best type of exposure; physically living in another country and experiencing the culture firsthand.

When I traveled abroad, I always made an effort to live like the locals versus hanging out with other foreigners. Integrating with local people helped me learn their culture quicker and, as an added benefit, it gained their respect. I was almost always treated like family. I took a similar approach when I traveled with my family. Since more than half of Malaysia's population is Muslim and I had previously had assignments in the Middle East, it was an opportunity for all of us to gain a deeper understanding of another religion. I shared what I had learned about Islam, and, from the start of our visit, we were immediately treated with mutual respect as Christians, which was drastically different from what was being conveyed by most media outlets. Likewise, they appreciated us making an effort to understand and respect their culture. It really underscored my dad's foundational lessons of respecting others. It has been applicable in every country I've visited.

Living like the locals presents a prime opportunity to put yourself in someone else's shoes, to see life from their point of view and potentially influence them to consider life from your point of view, expanding everyone's exposure beyond what they currently know. By immersing ourselves in the culture of Malaysia, local residents saw it as a sign of respect. They were more open and willing to share their culture and way of life when they saw someone who appreciated their country as more than a simple tourist location. They were also more comfortable asking questions about life in the US. Almost everyone wanted to know what it's like to live in America.

Even though I grew up poor, the level of poverty I witnessed in some of the countries I visited was deeper and more widespread. When I tried to explain it to my family, words couldn't describe the depth of poverty in ways that they could fully grasp. While living in Asia, my family got to see firsthand people living in extreme poverty in Malaysia, Thailand, and Indonesia—full families living under trees in boxes, people washing their clothes and bathing in mud holes where rainwater had settled, and small villages with no houses, only pieces of plywood on top of wooden stakes in the ground. The salaries of workers in some of these countries was less than $5 a week to feed a family of four. Despite their poor economic conditions, the citizens of these countries were some of the friendliest and happiest people we had ever met. Many people in the US correlate happiness with financial wealth. The mindset of people in these countries pressed my kids to look beyond the poverty on the surface, and they learned to see a different form of internal wealth. In turn, we genuinely represented ourselves as Americans who were truly interested in learning more about their culture, taking time to listen to their perspectives and not giving the impression that the American way was the only way. We didn't consider ourselves above them, and they rewarded us with their openness towards us.

In September 2009, my assignment in Malaysia was cut short after a little over a year due to an economic downturn. My manager was very accommodating with our move back to the US. He was sympathetic to the shortened assignment and allowed me to take six weeks of vacation before returning to work in the US. That window of flexibility launched a journey for us that most people on earth never get to experience. From Malaysia we traveled to Mumbai, India. From Mumbai we traveled to Alexandria and Cairo, Egypt, where one of my Egyptian friends gave us a guided tour, including to the Great Pyramid of Giza where we rode horses and camels in the desert.

From Egypt we traveled to Italy where we visited the Roman Colosseum and other historical locations in Rome before traveling farther north to Florence. We took the train from Florence to Pisa to view the Leaning Tower before departing for Spain. We still hadn't fully recovered from the jet lag and decided to spend a little extra time in Spain. We took advantage of the additional downtime by relaxing at the beach on our last day. The beaches were crowded, and we didn't notice anything unusual until Ronnie Jr. quietly said, "Dad, why is that lady throwing the Frisbee with no clothes on!" We had ended up at a topless beach!

Soon we were off to France where we were greeted with a not-as-friendly welcome in Paris. After finally getting some directions from one friendly bus rider, we eventually made our way to the Eiffel Tower, another astonishing structure that we had only read about in books and seen on television. Unfortunately, due to the lack of hospitality we experienced, we decided to shorten our stay in France and extend our time in the Netherlands, our next destination, where we found the Dutch people to be very friendly and welcoming. After starting in Rotterdam and The Hague, we moved to Amsterdam, which was filled with history, culture, and character. Our boat rides through city canals and full day visit to the Van Gogh Museum were highly educational. However, it was the emotional walk through the Anne Frank House that created the most memorable experience for Ronnie Jr. and Jonathan.

Our extra days in the Netherlands finally helped us overcome our jet lag before flying to England. By the time we reached London, we had been traveling for over a month and were exhausted. Nevertheless, we wanted the boys to see the London Bridge and Big Ben. Ronnie Jr. also had a special request to visit Buckingham Palace. His sole purpose for wanting to visit was to see if he could entice one of the guards to flinch. After nearly 15 minutes of prodding, one of the guards winked. It was the highlight of the trip to England for Ronnie! We toured our list of locations, including St. Paul's Cathedral, before taking a train up the coast to chilly Edinburgh, Scotland.

After nearly six weeks of planes, trains, and automobiles, we traveled back to London for our return flight to Chicago. When we landed in Chicago, we all took a big sigh of relief to be back on US soil. We had literally traveled the world and visited places most people will never get to see firsthand! The magnitude didn't resonate with us until later when we received a note from Jonathan's teacher. The students were asked to talk about their experience over the summer. She said Jonathan had the best imagination of any first-grader she had taught. He told the class he had been snorkeling in Thailand, rode a camel to the Pyramids of Egypt, played in the tulip fields in the Netherlands, touched the Eiffel Tower, and had seen one of the guards wink at Buckingham Palace in London! We ended up showing her some photos during his parent-teacher conference. She was visibly embarrassed for assuming he wasn't being truthful. It was definitely hard to believe, and when the conference was over, we all looked at each other and burst into laughter. We were all thinking the same thing. Thank goodness Jonathan didn't tell the class he had seen ladies' boobs in Spain! #seetheworld, #globetrotters, #globalmindset, #makingitreal, #doersnottalkers, #lifetimeexperience, #tripofalifetime

Two Steps Forward, One Step Back

It's difficult to describe the mix of emotions, both highs and lows, we experienced after moving back home to Illinois. The United States is the most developed country in the world, and it's nearly impossible to appreciate all of the amenities we have until you've lived abroad. When our six-week vacation was over and the plane made its final descent into Chicago O'Hare airport, the feeling was surreal. We all exhaled and said a prayer the moment the wheels screeched onto the runway. After the nearly 14-month journey around the world, we were finally back on US soil.

For Ronnie Jr. and Jonathan, it was the start of the school year, and they quickly became acclimated in their schools and rekindled old friendships almost instantly. Their travels and experiences made them celebrities to some classmates, which helped them develop friendships quickly.

While the boys' repatriation was going very well, Gina and I were struggling. Prior to our move to Malaysia, our marriage had been rocky. Our continuity had progressively deteriorated for the better part of 10 years. We had tried counseling and short-term getaways, but the gains were not sustainable. We had discussed divorce before the move to Malaysia but hoped the assignment, in a totally new environment, would breathe new life into our marriage. It did superficially, but the happiness was short-lived.

Back in Illinois we no longer had a maid, as we had in Malaysia, to do all of our cooking, cleaning, laundry, grocery shopping, ironing, and other household tasks, and the responsibilities for those day-to-day tasks became sources of contention. There were other challenges as well, including our finances. My salary was 50% greater than when we had originally moved to Illinois, but it was not double as we had gotten accustomed to overseas, and, as another drawback, my company was no longer covering most of our expenses. We had to drastically reduce our spending in order to keep our budget in line, continue saving at a decent rate, and maintain some level of charitable donations. Budgeting was not an option; it was a requirement! We had to curb our spending, which was a bitter pill for all of us to swallow. After not making appreciable progress to get aligned on spending, I made an executive decision to take over the family finances. We could no longer afford the luxuries of golf every weekend, getting hair and nails done weekly, or eating out five nights a week.

The contentious environment created a tremendous amount of stress for both of us, and something had to give. I rarely made significant decisions when I was overly happy or overly sad—I waited until my mind was more settled. After laboring over the divorce decision for weeks, I believed a tiered approach was better than a drastic change. Smaller changes, either good or bad, are easier to digest than drastic changes. We had already been living in separate bedrooms for a couple of years as a first step. Our finances were beginning to recover with the strict adherence to the budget, so we had a bit more flexibility. We had also done our best to channel our focus on the well-being of the boys. Within a year of returning to the US, we filed for divorce. I moved into another home nearby and Gina and I started 50-50 joint custody.

When we mutually agreed to get the divorce, a heavy burden lifted off both our shoulders immediately. Ronnie Jr. and Jonathan had personally witnessed the distance between us and also wanted to see all of us in a happier place. They were not surprised when we told them about the divorce. It was a bittersweet realization and validation that the facade we had projected hadn't really convinced them anyway. After the divorce, Gina developed deeper friendships with a few people that lived in and around our neighborhood and focused on the boys during her free time. I focused heavily on work and spent as much of my free time with the boys as I could.

Divorce is never easy. At the same time, we must go through tough times occasionally if we want to improve. Decoupling our marriage, expectations, personal priorities, and preferences were necessary for both of us to continue growing at rates that fit who we were at the time. Neither trajectory was necessarily wrong, they were just different. The divorce gave Gina a chance to focus more on her aspirations, which included completing her master's degree, something she had started many years before. Knowing the challenges I had gone through over the years and recognizing how much my family had always supported my aspirations, I wanted nothing more than to see her reach her goals. I tried to be supportive in every way possible.

My thirst for continuous improvement had not diminished. The prior two years had demotivated me and I felt sedentary and complacent in some ways. After the divorce, I regained my focus and passion to improve. Getting the divorce felt like a step backwards, but it allowed all of us to take multiple steps forward.

Starting with the first day after the decision was made to get a divorce, I recommitted to stay true to who I was and, in many ways, get back to being myself. At times I had compromised my innate boundaries of being humble, compassionate, positive, optimistic, and progressive-minded. I don't thrive in negative environments, so my day-one commitment to being the best ex-husband on the planet, irrespective of how I felt I was treated, was crucial for my own well-being, and it set the pace for how I proceeded throughout the divorce and afterward. I thought back to when my parents split up, and I remembered how my dad always helped my mom and her new man and had treated them with respect. I know he did it for them and for me and my brothers to see that he lived by his words. Treating others with respect regardless of the circumstances was part of who he was, and I knew it was a part of who I was too. Meanwhile, living on my own, relieved of the burden of trying to salvage my marriage, I reached a height of happiness that I had only dreamt of. My time with the boys was the best that it had ever been, hanging out, doing home projects, and cooking together. It not only saved money but gave me a chance to spend quality time teaching the boys how to grill from the grill master!

The quality time with the boys, getting back to who I was, and being in a less stressful environment was life-changing on multiple levels. I had always challenged myself to get better, work harder, and continuously question the status quo. The relentless pursuit of being better tomorrow than yesterday is not for everyone. As I plowed through the walls that blocked a better life for my family, I did everything in my power to remain considerate, mindful of others, tactful, and unselfish. But admittedly, I could have lessened the stress on all of us had I recognized how my drive and motivation affected my family.

While there are obvious benefits to being extremely driven, constantly working to develop new skills, and always searching for ways to do things better, also has its downside. It can create a feeling of perpetual discomfort. Purposely choosing to be out of your comfort zone is not for everyone, and perhaps not everyone in my family was in agreement with constantly striving for knowledge and improvement. We all have different appetites for continuous growth, and although I realized it, I wasn't always considerate of the disparity on a day-to-day basis. A lesson learned is to recognize everyone handles discomfort and growth differently. Some people are content with the status quo, and for them, that is okay. #bestexhusbandever, #treatpeoplefair, #mindfuldecisionmaking, #dontbevindictive

Caught in a Terrorist Attack

Nearly six years after the divorce, I had remarried and was living a wonderful and exciting life. Kayla, my wife, had never traveled outside of the US before we were married. We quickly got her a passport and started traveling the globe. In our first two years together, we had visited seven different countries in Asia and Europe. It was a blessing to re-experience these countries through her eyes. She embraced the approach of living like the locals, learning a little of the language and respecting the different cultures. She always prepared for trips by doing research ahead of time and interacting with people we met as if they were long-time family members. Our intent was to always present a positive image as Americans traveling abroad.

In June 2016, we planned for a two-week vacation in Malaysia. The initial flight included a layover in Istanbul, Turkey. I had visited Istanbul several times and always admired its beauty. When we arrived at Ataturk Airport in Istanbul, we contemplated taking a quick tour around the city. We had an eight-hour layover, which gave us a small but workable window of time. After some debate, we scrapped the idea of a quick city tour and decided to hang out in the business class lounge. The food selection, service, and atmosphere were great, so we relaxed and planned more details for Malaysia.

After several hours watching the soccer match on television, we heard several pops that sounded like firecrackers. Kayla asked, "Is that from the soccer match?" I immediately realized it was gunfire and told Kayla to run! She was stunned so I grabbed her hand and started dragging her away from the noise. At that instant, there was a loud explosion! The force was so strong that it blew out ceiling tiles above us and sprayed the walls and ceilings with glass and blood. We were frantically running to the opposite corner of the lounge when more automatic weapon fire erupted, shattering the glass wall near where we had been sitting. Like a scene from a movie, there we were in a small room walled in glass that, though only large enough to hold seven or eight people, was now crammed with 25 to 30 screaming people. We didn't know if we were going to live or die!

Amid all of this chaos, I felt terrible that I had put Kayla in this situation. I knew about some of the turmoil in Turkey before our trip, but I never expected anything like this to happen. After another loud explosion, more people started surging and rushing into the small room we were crammed in. Kayla was consoling a young lady on the floor who was completely limp from fear. Kayla was strong, even as her lips and hands trembled. She held the quivering lady's hand to console her. I was determined to shield Kayla and do everything I had to do to keep her alive.

We didn't know if the terrorists were directly outside the door or not. People were screaming as if the threat was coming directly toward us. My hands were shaking uncontrollably but

I was able to call Ronnie Jr. to let him know that we were trapped in a terrorist attack and that we were probably going to die. I called several of our close family members and friends, but Ronnie Jr. and my boss in New Jersey were the only people I got on the phone, primarily due to the eight-hour time difference. We all started praying in the room, asking that God protect us from the terrorists. There were Muslims, Christians, Hindus, and others all praying together in the same room. I asked Ronnie Jr. to call the family, including Kayla's family members, and let them know our situation. My phone battery was almost dead so we said goodbye, not knowing if it was the last time we would ever speak to each other.

Even with my level of fear, I was evaluating options to get out. I made my way out of the small room and asked staff members if there was an alternate exit. One person was too shook to speak and the other was frantically dialing on her cell phone, ignoring my question. They were both young and not in a frame of mind to help others. I looked around for a safer place in case the terrorists made their way to the lounge, but unfortunately most areas were walled in glass. As I surveyed the lounge, there was an option to hide behind shelving and other pushcarts in the kitchen area. Kayla and I walked to a corridor leading through the kitchen and supply room to the other side of the lounge. One of the senior staffers directed people to move to the other side of the lounge. We quickly moved and nestled behind a minibar. The smell of explosives made it hard to breathe.

Within minutes after hiding behind the minibar, I received a text message from my company's global security leader. He immediately started giving updates on what was going on with the details he had. There appeared to be three terrorists and two had already been killed. One was still in the parking lot shooting into the building. As we were talking, more automatic weapon fire started piercing the glass structure behind the minibar in the area that the staffer had just instructed us to move to. Immediately, the staffer yelled for everyone to run back to the other side of the room. He had just led us to the side where the parking lot was located and in the direct sight of the terrorist.

As we started back through the corridor, I noticed huge bundles of towels that we could possibly hide behind. I quickly checked the weight of them and the pushcarts. Seeing that I was trying to figure out a plan, people started asking me what I thought we should do. I didn't have a clue, but I wasn't going to sit idle without making an effort for us to survive. There was a lady in a wheelchair that simply couldn't react quickly to the changing situation, so I asked Kayla and the lady in the wheelchair if they wanted me to barricade them behind the big bundles of towels. The lady was okay with it, but Kayla immediately said "NO! I am going wherever you are going." I told the lady in the wheelchair that if I heard any more gunfire, I would physically take her out of the wheelchair and barricade her behind the bundles of towels. She and her daughter were very appreciative and were ready to go when one of the staffers started yelling for everyone's attention. He said the situation was under control and all the terrorists had been killed.

As much as I wanted to simply take his word that everything was over, there were still many unknowns. We didn't know if he was part of the plot or if he was indeed a good guy. I am sure everyone in there was suspicious. As we stood there listening to his message, he turned on a big-screen TV that showed all the carnage and blood that was in the arrival hall. I could immediately start piecing together some of the sounds we had heard earlier. The initial gunshots that sounded like a firecracker was the security guard killing the first terrorist. He noticed a terrorist running with a machine gun, so he shot him, and, as the terrorist was taking his last breath, he was scrambling to pull the string to detonate the explosive. That was the first explosion we heard. The second terrorist was standing in the arrival hall gunning down women, children, everyone he could find.

As we gained more confidence that the staffer had legitimate information, we started to settle down a bit. Then several military people came into the lounge to give us a briefing. Although they were military dressed in uniform, it was still unnerving considering what we had gone through. They were heavily armed with machine guns and pistols. They told us they would take care of us. The staffer said not to worry, everyone would be taken care of and taken to a hotel for the night because they were going to shut down the airport. In the process of shutting down the airport everyone needed to go through the immigration line and have their passports checked. It was a scary thought to leave the shelter of the airport and go out into the open city. As we gathered in the lounge, I noticed a lady wearing a hijab. She had done an excellent job of reuniting kids separated from their parents during the chaos. We approached her and her family and told her that we had seen and were proud of what she had done. Recognizing that she was Muslim, I asked her husband if he was okay with me shaking her hand. We want to always respect cultures, and he had no objections. The entire family started tearing up and was very appreciative for the recognition. Several family members gave us a big hug.

The staffer from the lounge asked us to line up so we could leave in an orderly fashion and head to the immigration checkpoint area. As we started moving towards the area, we saw thousands of people being herded into five or six lines in the emigration hall. It was chaotic at best. As we finally made our way to the hall, there was screaming and people jumping over one another trying to exit the area. Kayla and I pushed our way closer to the immigration agents where we saw many middle-aged men jumping the barricades to skip the line. It was a mentality of "every man for himself" rather than being considerate of others who had been standing in the line for what felt like hours. Once Kayla and I got within about ten yards of the immigration officers, people started pressing into us from behind. I had had enough at that point and held my arms out to grab the bars blocking the line. The look on my face was clear—do NOT touch my arm! Enough was enough! Kayla recognized what I was doing, and she started helping adults with children and elderly people move to the area that I was blocking. Neither one of us could stomach seeing the adult men jump over women and children to skip the line.

The air conditioner was not working and some of the elderly people were sweating and feeling faint. Kayla was asking people if they had extra water to give them. She was also consoling some of the little kids that were screaming. We both held babies as parents started moving toward the immigration checkpoint. It was a tough scene for people that had already gone through a lot.

As we inched closer to the immigration officers, still with about a dozen people ahead of us, others started trying to barge in from the rear. But they could see the look on my face and wouldn't dare touch my arm. The immigration officer spotted what Kayla and I were doing and, initially, I thought he was angry with us, but he gave us a thumbs-up for helping control the crowd and allowing the families with children to move through first. Kayla said she was okay waiting until more women and children had moved through ahead of us. After several families came through, the immigration officer flagged for the other people to get out of the way and let Kayla and me walk to the desk next. He saw how long we had been standing there, shepherding people through the line. He thanked us both when we got there and said Americans are good people! With everything going on, it let us know that we were doing the right things despite the situation.

As we walked past the immigration desk, we were nearly brought to tears with all the blood and carnage that we saw. Cardboard was placed on the floors to make a walkway over the pools of blood. It was like nothing we have ever seen, and the smell was something I will never forget. We walked for nearly 100 yards to the exit and noticed that none of the escalators were working. There were dozens of families with strollers waiting to go downstairs but couldn't because the escalators were not working. I asked Kayla if she was okay with me helping bring strollers down the stairs. We both wanted to get out of there in a hurry, but we couldn't in good conscience let these people stand there, knowing they couldn't get down the stairs. I told them that I would help carry the strollers down the stairs. Some clenched onto the handles every step of the way, not knowing me from anyone else. They were still worried even as Kayla assured them that we only wanted to help. As people lined up to be taken to hotels, we made more runs to get strollers down the stairs.

Finally, Kayla and I got on one of the buses, and I asked about the plan. The staffer inside had said they would take care of us, but we didn't know what that meant and there didn't seem to be a clear plan. Even still, we felt some sense of comfort that we were heading to a hotel. The further we drove the more we started feeling as if there was not really a plan, and about 30 minutes into the bus ride we realized the extent of the plan. They were simply getting survivors away from the airport. They just put us on buses, sending some north, some south, some east, and some west and dropping us in nearby cities to find our own hotels.

Fortunately for us, we quickly found the Taksim Gonen Hotel, which looked reasonable. When we went to the counter, the attendant didn't ask us any questions. He said, 'I have a room for you, and I will give it to you at our cheapest price." He saw that we didn't have any luggage, only our backpacks, and also what we had gone through. Thank God he was a good person and treated us fairly. After getting to our room and showering, it took us a little time to settle down. My mind couldn't stop replaying what had happened and what I needed to do to get Kayla out of Turkey. I felt helpless and couldn't imagine how she felt. Suddenly, it dawned on me that we needed to schedule our flight for the next day if the airport reopened. I hopped out of bed and called United Airlines. Fortunately, they were able to book us on an evening flight out of Istanbul back to the US the next day.

Kayla and I were both fine canceling our vacation and flying back home. Our plans were set for the next day and we were able to get a decent night of sleep. When we went to the breakfast area of the hotel the next morning, the view of the city was beautiful. Both of us were in awe of the beauty and disappointed that we did not get a chance to explore it under better circumstances. We also realized that if we had quickly toured the city instead of waiting in the lounge, we would have likely returned and been standing in the immigration line at the same time terrorists opened fire and slaughtered people. We might easily have been killed!

Shortly after breakfast we went to the Turkish Airlines location near the hotel to see if we could get on an earlier flight. As we sat in the office area waiting in a very long line to book a ticket, I started feeling uncomfortable with the vulnerable situation we were in. I grabbed Kayla's hand and said we were leaving without explaining my thoughts or getting her worked up again. I waited until we got back to the hotel before explaining to her that I would rather us quickly get past immigration at the airport and sit in the lounge for five more hours versus waiting in that vulnerable office trying to get an earlier flight. Terrorists knew foreigners were trying to get out of the country and needed to re-book their flights. There was no security at the Turkish Airlines office so if a terrorist wanted to come in, they could kill everyone in the office in a matter of minutes, whereas the airport was probably the safest place in Turkey at that moment.

We got back to the hotel, quickly packed our items, and took a taxi back to Ataturk Airport. There were dozens of military police all over the airport grounds. We scurried out of the taxi, passed through immigration, and headed toward the same lounge where we were held up during the terrorist attack. They had cleaned up a lot of the blood and debris from the terrorist attack and re-opened the lounge. As we sat in the airport near the seats that we were sitting in before, we noticed bullet holes in the glass in front of our seats. Had we stayed in our seats the day before, we would have been hit. Fortunately, we were able to get on our flight to Frankfurt, Germany, and back to the US unharmed physically but scarred for life mentally from the experience.

Despite the horror we had faced, there was so much positive in the situation with us helping people and hearing them say, "Americans, you are my brother and my sister! Thank you!" In spite of the danger that we were in, it was innate for me to look for ways to help others even while looking to keep myself and Kayla safe in this frightening situation. Both of us felt that even if we did not make it out alive, we would have died giving comfort and assistance to others around us. The Muslim lady who helped separated children reunite with their parents also saw a need greater than her own, and I was grateful to have spoken to her family and recognized her efforts. By the grace of God, we survived the terrorist attack and were able to step up and help others feel safe and voluntarily act as facilitators to assist them in getting out of the airport. I will never forget the terror we felt, but I will also never forget the feeling of purpose, that I was there, able to help and serve others in a time of great need. #knowyourexits, #expecttheunexpected

Links to terrorist attack in Istanbul, Turkey (GRAPHIC CONTENT WARNING:

1. https://nbcnews.to/3dwfsAR
2. https://nbcnews.to/3x9Q6R6
3. https://bbc.in/3dwfOYd

###

HOW TO CHANGE
THE WORLD

It seems surreal to reach the closing chapters of the book! I feel comfortable that readers have gotten to know me by this point. I was challenged to stay true to who I am, and a large part of that is to acknowledge the contributions of others in my successes. People helped me in every phase of my journey and, although this book is largely about my life, there is no denying the immeasurable impact of encouragement, opportunities, and support from others.

My hope is to encourage readers to purposely seek out one or two Hidden Gems who are in the early stages of their journey and actively come up with ways to help them realize their potential. Keep in mind that Hidden Gems likely will not know their true potential and may even be resistant if help is offered in ways that require them to put skin in the game. Another plan is to help Hidden Gems learn lessons from a different set of challenges. Many of us are grounded in belief that "all challenges make us stronger." While this may be true, it is also a flawed way of thinking. Many Hidden Gems are inherently under constant duress from life-or-death challenges. Many carry catastrophic ramifications from their neighborhoods, social settings, and shared living situations. Yes, people grow from being challenged, but there are more reasonable ways to learn the same valuable lessons without, for example, a Hidden Gem having no option other than to continue living in a house where drug deals are occurring when they vehemently oppose the activities. They can learn a valuable lesson by a Gem Seeker finding a creative way for them to earn a different, less dangerous living arrangement.

Don't Let Perfection Get in the Way of Getting Better

I don't know of any problem in life that requires a perfect solution, and we shouldn't let a quest for perfection, or waiting for the exact right time, paralyze us to a point of doing nothing. In the spirit of continuous improvement, Gem Seekers should take the lead in helping Hidden Gems make incremental improvements, primarily because Gem Seekers have the advantage of knowing better. We should assume that Hidden Gems don't know how to build an improvement plan and may not recognize opportunities even when they are presented to them. Many are constantly in crisis, working multiple jobs, struggling with school and home situations, and largely living in survival mode. Even if we have never faced the challenges they have, Gem Seekers must be empathetic and communicate on a level that Hidden Gems can understand. Interacting with Hidden Gems can be challenging, and there is not a "one size fits all" approach. Gem Seekers can make an impact just by being a living example of something different. For example, I saw how the Gardners were different from me. They had a pantry full of food. They had steak for dinner. They had a nice house, appliances, and running water. I wanted all those things, but I didn't know how to get there from where I was, living in my car. But they were willing to show me, to help me create a better situation where my life could improve.

A number of years ago when I lived in an apartment, I had a conversation with a well-intentioned person in my community, Mrs. Barbara, about helping a young single mom, Tina, who was struggling to make ends meet. Tina wasn't receiving any support from the father of her two sons, which exacerbated her situation. Mrs. Barbara had given Tina several hundred dollars and encouraged her to get a better job so her boys wouldn't be another generation on government assistance. When Tina asked Mrs. Barbara for another small loan, she was convinced that Tina was using her for handouts, wasn't interested in giving up her government assistance, and wasn't trying to better herself. Mrs. Barbara's intentions were good, but her conversation with Tina went off the rails quickly. She told Tina that she felt sorry for the boys having to suffer but that Tina's perfect solution was to get a degree and press charges against the father for not paying child support.

I thought about the situation and felt like I was in a position to potentially help. I saw Tina at our community mailbox building about two weeks later, around the middle of October, and asked her how things were going. She gave me a similar version of what Mrs. Barbara had told me. She said her ex-boyfriend wasn't paying her child support and she was struggling to make ends meet. All of her bills were past due, on reduced payment plans, and her credit was shot so she couldn't get a loan. Most of her conversation sounded truthful on the surface from her perspective, but there were all kinds of red flags for me! I wanted to ask more questions to understand the situation better, but I could tell she was frustrated and exhausted from work, so I decided to wait for a better time to get more details.

With Halloween approaching, I knew there would be another chance for us to talk in more detail. Kids participated in a hayride through the complex, giving parents time to socialize. When I saw Tina this time, she was in a much better mood. I was eager to learn more about her situation but was also particular to ask in ways that didn't cause her to get defensive. I imagine she had been asked the same questions numerous times about her personal life, so I wanted to simply learn more from a general conversation rather than making her feel like she was being quizzed to get more details. She told me about Mrs. Barbara voluntarily giving her a total of $365 but she was determined to pay back every dollar of it. To me, that was a great sign because it meant she wasn't looking for a hand-out, nor was she trying to take advantage of Mrs. Barbara. Tina saw the money from Mrs. Barbara as a loan to be repaid and not a gift with no strings attached.

☀ **Words of Wisdom** ☀
"If a person keeps up with exactly how much they owe you, it's a good sign that they probably intend to pay you back."
- John Stallworth, Sr.

As Tina continued explaining how she wanted to go back to school to complete her degree, secure a better job to get off government assistance, and give her boys a better life, I was impressed by the passion and determination in her voice. At the same time, she was overwhelmed by the commitment to make it all happen. She couldn't connect the dots on a realistic path to get from point A (her current situation), to points B, C, and so on when she would have a degree and they were all living a better life (point F or G). Her situation resonated with me, and I was compelled to help her figure out a plan. She needed smaller, more manageable steps to make incremental improvements versus working toward a grand but generic plan that sounded perfect on paper but was too broad to execute.

The more we spoke, the more opportunities came to light. We strategized for hours that night sitting on her deck, jotting down the details of a more granular plan as her sons played with other kids in the complex. I learned that her ex-boyfriend had gotten laid off from one of his jobs but was still paying Tina's car payment and auto insurance. He was also paying for the boys' health insurance and paying for most of their school clothes and fees. The car payment alone was more than what he would have been required to pay in child support had she simply taken him to court. It was a surprising twist to learn that the boyfriend was doing more than what was required. Tina admitted that her emotions from their breakup had blinded her appreciation for his generosity. It was easier and "technically" truthful for her to simply tell others that he wasn't paying child support versus owning up to her own underlying issues.

Tina was only two semesters away from completing her nursing degree, but she had previously decided to drop out of school and was working a second job for a while, planning to re-enroll after paying off some of her debts. As we continued to talk through her plan to make incremental improvements, all was going along well until we had to address the elephant in the room, her smoking habit. When I mentioned that she should consider giving up cigarettes, she became defensive. I explained to her that perception is extremely important, especially when you're hoping other people will help you out. If they feel like you are trying to beat the system and get something for nothing, they will probably walk away. She acknowledged spending nearly as much per month on cigarettes as she did on electricity! With her agreement to temporarily stop smoking until she completed the two semesters, I agreed to pay the past due portion of her credit card, which was about $150. I also agreed to watch her sons one night a week for two hours so she could take one of her remaining courses. Mrs. Barbara agreed to watch them one night a week as well. Tina agreed to some other basic cost-saving tactics including turning the lights off when she left the apartment, not leaving the television on all night (which I could hear), not eating out more than once a month, paying her credit card on time, and not spending money that she didn't have in the rough budget we put together.

The first semester went by quickly and, for the final semester, I changed jobs and transferred back to Illinois, but I kept up with Tina. Mrs. Barbara watched the boys most of the time, but Tina also let her ex-boyfriend keep them periodically. After nearly nine months of grinding it out in school and working two jobs, Tina completed her nursing degree, got off government assistance, caught up on her bills, and her sons were spending quality time with their dad. The plan that we put together on Tina's deck that Halloween night wasn't perfect. She was waiting for the perfect timing to restart school and, as a result, had sat out for over a year with no real urgency to resume. She assumed she didn't make enough money to get by, but once she saw where she could make some changes in her budget, she was able to pay her bills on time. Sometimes we just need to get started instead of waiting for a perfect moment in time, which rarely ever happens. I really cannot over-stress the importance of incremental improvements. It is an approach to life ALL of us can benefit from.

About six months after Tina graduated, I received a letter in the mail from her with a $150 check. The money I had given her was a gift, not a loan, and I didn't expect it to be paid back, but she was determined to send it, though I never cashed the check. Tina also let me know in the letter that Mrs. Barbara had passed away, but not before Tina paid back the $365 she owed her! At her funeral, Mrs. Barbara's husband said she couldn't stop talking about how proud she was that Tina proved her assumptions wrong.

Mrs. Barbara did have a genuine desire to help Tina. She had good intentions, but the advice she gave was so broad and generic that it didn't resonate with Tina. Mrs. Barbara also did what many people do—she simply took Tina's comments at face value without asking probing questions. The boyfriend sounded like a deadbeat dad, when in reality he was paying more than what he was obligated to pay. He also wanted to spend more time with the boys, but their emotions got in the way of doing what was in the best interest of the boys. Tina was also spending over $400 per month eating out, buying cigarettes, and entertaining friends. When I paid her past-due credit card bill, I paid it directly to the credit card company versus simply giving Tina the cash. We worked out a simple plan with small, incremental steps, allowing Tina to track her progress. The plan included some sacrifices and contributions from Tina; not everything was given to her. Finally, Tina had agreed to show me her income and expenses. I trusted her to be truthful about her financials, but I also wanted to verify them until she was out of the woods.

I have repeatedly mentioned the value of exposure, seeing things firsthand, helping shepherd Hidden Gems through a path to earn their way, and not letting preconceived notions jade our opinions. These are important because, more often than not, young people will emulate what they see at home and in their neighborhoods, communities, and cities unless there are outsiders that steer them in different directions. Tina's kids learned a ton during the little time I was with them, and so did Tina. Before we put together our plan, Tina would call the maintenance department at the apartment if a light bulb needed changing. She would call them if the doorknob screws became loose. If they knocked a hole in the sheetrock wall, they'd claim it was already damaged when they moved in and they wanted it repaired. There was almost no sense of accountability. Her two sons witnessed this consistently as the way to get things done. They saw it as the landlord's responsibility to make all repairs, and even do a little extra when they accidentally knocked a hole in the wall. Without intervention, her sons would likely treat their future landlords the same way when they grew up.

During the few months I was around Tina and her sons, I let her sons remove the glass globes and change several bulbs. They were so nervous about dropping the glass, but they did just fine. When they removed the bulb, I showed all three of them the wattage and voltage on the bulb and taught them a little background behind it. I showed all of them how to use a Phillips-head screwdriver and even how to patch a hole in the drywall. A few days after the patch had dried, we sanded it, got a small container of paint from the office, and made the wall look good as new.

What I discovered is that all three of them were excited to be a part of making the repairs. Their perceived laziness was mostly the result of their limited mindset (that's the way Tina grew up and she continued doing the same when she was on her own). They all had the ability to do so much more when given a chance. We all tend to fall into the trap of thinking the way we do things is the right way or the only way. It just takes a little willingness to look deeper, ask questions, and be open to trying a different way that may work even better.

🪨 Cracks in The Wall 🪨

*There are inherent risks when trying to find the right balance between setting extremely high goals that are virtually impossible to reach versus setting challenging stretch/high-value targets that are attainable. But few risks have a greater return on investment than developing yourself if you are a Hidden Gem, or someone else if you are a Gem Seeker, to make the greatest difference possible in the world. **It's worth***

the risk to invest in opportunities to make positive change.
Making these choices will rarely be easy, no matter what side
of the wall you're on.

Second Chances Are a First Step

There is a saying that first impressions are lasting. For most people, including me, this has proven to be true over the years. It's a challenge to not quickly process the first thing we see and form an opinion. For Hidden Gems, this can be a killer. To be honest, I've struggled to not make immediate judgments about the way someone speaks, how they dress, and even how they approach problems. I've also been in countless situations where people have judged me and made an immediate assessment about my abilities based on a single data point such as a task that I did or didn't do well, a brief introduction to a contact, or a job interview.

In some cases, a first impression works to our advantage, and in other cases, unfortunately, we don't ever get another chance. After I completed my MBA, I was hungry for a new and challenging job role. About a month after graduating, a former HR director called me about a global marketing position within my company. It was a great opportunity for me but there were a number of unknowns. The position was in the photovoltaic part of the company, a technology I knew almost nothing about. I also didn't know the hiring manager or her style, and I didn't have any marketing or profit and loss (P/L) experience. I was given three days to prepare for the biggest interview of my career.

I started doing research directly after our call and learned that the hiring manager was a vice president, was tough on her team, had a direct communication style, and was next in line to be president and CEO of the division. Anxiety set in quickly. I tossed and turned most of the night until I was awakened by the phone ringing at 7 o'clock the next morning. It was the vice president calling to interview me! She said "Ron, I know our interview is not scheduled until later in the week, but I need to get it over with and see if you are right for the job or not."

She asked me two quick questions. First, "If I gave you the job role right now, what's the first thing you'd do as global marketing leader?" As I struggled to get out of bed and quietly clear my throat, she asked me "What do you know about the macro and micro trends in the photovoltaic market?" I scrambled to get up the stairs to my home-office computer where I kept my notes. Just as I reached the top of the stairs, she said "Ron, I realize you were asleep, but I needed to get on with my schedule. It was good talking with you, but I can usually tell quickly if someone is a good fit or not and I don't think you are a good fit for this role." It was barely 7:05 AM and the interview was over. It was like trying to hit a 100-mph fastball with a broomstick. I had failed miserably and, even more disappointing, I felt I had let down the HR director who had highly recommended me for the role.

"Always start preparing for an interview the moment you hear about it. The hiring manager will be remarkably impressed if they call you earlier and you're able to respond with thoroughness and clarity."
-Ronnie Stallworth, Sr.

In less than five minutes, in an unscheduled interview, she had decided I wasn't a good fit for the job and ended the interview. As harsh as it was, I may not have been a perfect fit for the role at the time. However, I knew I had the ability to grow into a capable global marketing leader. But her speed in deciding to not allow me to respond and not hire me kept us from getting to know each other and seeing the potential of what we could create working together on the same team. That setback taught me, among other things, that even highly intelligent and successful corporate executives sometimes frame their decisions into quick discrete decisions such as yes or no, go or no-go, or right or wrong, based on limited information. This was important because it forced me to prepare more before meetings and develop a more concise communication style. Hidden Gems must be better prepared because they are not always polished, and their first impressions may not be stellar. There are also preconceived notions that they may not be high performers, which means they'll have less time to show their value.

❧ **Hidden Gem Moment** ❧
*Hidden Gems should not be surprised or bitter about being challenged more than others. **These extra challenges are opportunities to put our true abilities on display.** View them as positive ways to improve and show our value!*

Following the interview, I thought about the questions she asked and how I should have responded to them, and then I developed a rough plan to mold myself into a solid candidate for that job role. I scheduled a meeting with my mentor, Norv Givens, to help me prepare for the next opportunity. He had recently been promoted to president of another division in the company. During our conversation, Norv offered me a similar global marketing role in his division. It also included full profit and loss responsibility and, as a bonus, it involved maintenance and reliability, a sector that I was familiar with from previous job roles. Norv knew a lot about my learning style and work ethic from our mentoring sessions. He was also aware that I didn't have any experience running an entire business. However, the business had not turned a profit since company purchased it, and Norv knew I'd performed well in the past with a little guidance to get started.

Once I was in the role, I immediately started assessing the situation and saw that we were trying to build up too many products at once, and so we refined the portfolio of offerings. My team developed a business plan and go-to-market strategies, and we coordinated with the Research and Development team to make sure all the products communicated across the same platform. I constantly showed appreciation to my team along the way for their creativity, willingness to work longer hours to meet the launch window, and openness to think differently than they had before. We hit our launch window a month earlier than planned and started raking in sales. By the end of my first year in the role, we were the only one of six sub-businesses that met our annual operating plan, and we turned a profit for the first time. It proved to me that I was capable of being a general manager for a business, but it took Norv, an advocate and Gem Seeker, to see more potential in me than I saw in myself.

Hidden Gems might need a second or third chance before progress is made, and often Hidden Gems need additional encouragement and a higher vision to get started. I probably wouldn't have interviewed so poorly on the initial opportunity had I not been abruptly awakened by the random call from the vice president. However, the ramification wasn't a killer for me. I took ownership for not being prepared, even with the odd way it occurred. My positive and accountable approach helped prepare me for the next interview where I did win the job. I got back up from my stumble and proved my worth to the company.

Sometimes, people that don't have previous experience in a particular area can bring innovative solutions and approaches that others don't see. Hiring the same type of candidate over and over will likely yield results similar to what the company or department has seen in the past. The person who was eventually hired as the photovoltaic global marketing leader was a candidate that had previous global marketing experience. He needed virtually no training, and once he was on board, he ran the business much like his predecessors, with no significant change in the business model.

Norv knew my potential as a leader. He also knew that I perform better when I have a rough description of what my leader's vision is versus only providing a blank sheet of paper as a starting point, and he was more than willing to provide me with that information. There are many ways to get to the same destination. If I know the destination (vision), I can figure out how to get there and typically bring more value in the journey because I am not stuck in the ways it has been done before. When I initially took the role, several existing team members constantly bombarded me with the phrase "This is the way we've always done it," and I politely but purposely discarded most of what they told me. After all, the business had never turned a profit when it was operated the way they had always done it. What I brought to the role was a different way of thinking, fresh perspective, and diversity of thought in the way things had always been done versus being just like the other candidates, and, given the chance, I could have done that in the photovoltaic division as well.

When offered a job that you are not familiar with, you must balance the competing priorities of getting up to speed quickly based on what your current team tells you versus using your creativity to think of different approaches to run the business, develop products, segment the market, etc. The latter may take a little more time to materialize, and you may repeat some mistakes of the past, but the upside potential can be great!

Life is not always fair, and Hidden Gems won't always get jobs they are capable of doing, primarily because they don't look like traditional candidates. Some executives are under so much pressure to make a quick decision that they overlook the potential in a candidate that isn't as polished as they are accustomed to seeing. Hidden Gems are rarely polished in their current state.

Hidden Gems will almost always have a steeper learning curve due to their limited background, lack of exposure, lower confidence and, in some cases, having to overcome competing priorities in their personal lives such as not having reliable transportation. Each of these factors creates layers of discomfort that must be managed to be successful. Gem Seekers and prospective Gem Seekers must plan for Hidden Gems to have missteps as they embark into uncharted waters, and in subsequent phases of their progression along the way. The reality is, we all make mistakes during trial-and-error situations and when we're stretched to learn something entirely new. Gem Seekers and Hidden Gems must agree on ways to minimize the negative impact of their mistakes to create a softer landing if they fall along the journey. Honest and open communication factor into this equation for all parties involved.

Character Cultivates Opportunity

I typically have six to eight people that I mentor at any given time. Most of them are within a year of graduating with their engineering degree. A question I always ask each mentee is, what will differentiate you from the other dozens of engineering candidates that apply for the same job role? Almost all of them say I should hire them because of their good grades, they really want the job, or their willingness to work hard if they get the role, which equates to almost no differentiation. On a few rare occasions, I've had a mentee say, "Because I treat people fairly, I'm going to quickly learn from my mistakes, and I want to be in a position to help others once I'm on board." To those rare candidates, I've usually said "You're hired" on the spot, even when we were not in an open interview.

People with a combination of integrity, character, honesty and passion are held in higher esteem and given more opportunities. These attributes are important to me personally because they were the cornerstones of my dad's approach to life and the way he parented us. His advice to put them out front in my decision-making process has been a differentiator for me over the years. When I've missed the mark and made decisions that didn't incorporate all three characteristics, I self-corrected enough times that I gained trust. It seems counterintuitive in some ways, but when I proactively acknowledged my mistakes, mentors who valued my genuineness emerged and gave me additional opportunities to prove my value. They knew I had set a high standard for myself even though I fell short at times.

By expecting more of myself than others did of me, and by setting my standards for good quality work at a higher level than what was required, I was rewarded. In some instances, I was the least experienced candidate for opportunities, but I succeeded because I was a lower risk option than someone who had more experience but had a poor work ethic. My job evaluations routinely said I had the right foundation to build success. In business terminology, my managers said I had a lot of runway, which refers to hiring a candidate that doesn't necessarily have all of the required experience at the moment, but they have the right attributes and capacity to grow into the role.

There is no substitute for treating people fairly in our personal and professional lives, even when no one is watching us. Doing so is an indicator of our character, which is more vulnerable now than ever. An unfortunate consequence of social media and the speed at which information is shared is sometimes that information is incorrect. Fewer people are taking the time to validate the authenticity of what they hear. I have heard some people say they don't care what others think about them, but I don't believe them. I don't know of anyone who wants their reputation tarnished, especially if it is done unfairly. I have always wanted people, especially my children, to see me in a positive light, trust what I say, and physically see me treating people with respect. I fall short at times, but I still strive for integrity, character, and honesty in my decisions, and I also encourage people in my world to do the same. I want to do things in such a way that my dad, and my kids, would be proud!

☼ **Words of Wisdom** ☼
**"The true test of a man's character is what he
does when no one is watching."**
-John Wooden

Different Forms of Wealth

Improving the world that we live in has a lot to do with our perspective. Whereas not many would deliberately choose to live a life of poverty, there are lessons in those circumstances that can be utilized in other areas of life. Paying attention to people and events around me has taught me that there are significant amounts of *unrecognized* wealth in unexpected places. We don't see it because we are conditioned to focus on what we want but don't have. There is a wealth of exposure that my poor living conditions provided. Had I not physically experienced the conditions firsthand, there is absolutely nothing I could do today to duplicate the same level of appreciation for what I have accomplished. That phase of my life helps me appreciate my life today, the life I worked hard for and earned.

Not having the financial means to purchase store-bought items helped me develop skills to identify alternatives, some of which were essentially free. I also learned the art of recognizing value in items that others saw as useless. Some of my most rewarding times took place at the local landfill where people discarded unwanted items. I would strategically pick through piles of trash to identify items that I would repair and reuse or sell for extra cash. This resourcefulness helps me to look at things, even situations, twice whereas others might disregard them at first glance.

I gained a lot of valuable lessons from not having running water in my house. It gave me a wealth of compassion for people in similar situations. When I wasn't able to take baths on a regular basis, I learned a lot about people and their lack of empathy. Other kids laughed at me for being smelly. In the process, I learned who to trust and who not to trust. It helped toughen my skin to handle criticism better as an adult. As a bonus, the lack of hot water on my skin is probably the reason I don't have wrinkles like other people my age!

Washing old milk jugs to refill with water at our neighbor's outdoor faucet taught me the value of having my own source of basic amenities. During the winter months when the outdoor water pipes froze, I learned prioritization. Only having enough water for drinking and cooking meant going several days without taking a bath.

The first time I took an actual shower was at Murphy High School at the age of 17. It was an amazing feeling, but it wasn't until I turned 19 years old and got my first apartment that I really realized how blessed I was. It was the first time I lived in a place that had an indoor toilet and personal shower. The feelings of accomplishment and appreciation were indescribable and validated the hard work and sacrifices I had made. The simple act of taking a shower alone in a bathroom where I could shut the door or pressing a button on my refrigerator to get a glass of water were luxuries that I'll never take for granted.

I wouldn't change how shy I was growing up. It gave me a wealth of caution and definitely kept me out of trouble. I struggled to fit in with other kids due to my low self-esteem. However, the alone time gave me a chance to learn more about myself, including how to look inward for understanding versus depending on others to define who I was. The lack of self-confidence during my impressionable teenage years kept me from getting into many risky activities. Some of my peers weren't so fortunate and landed in jail.

My shyness caused me to avoid getting involved with girls too soon. Sometimes girls openly laughed at me. They saw me as a poor, shy, dumb kid. But that isolation from girls, and my fear of them, also kept me from getting anyone pregnant as a teenager. Some of the girls actively tried to get pregnant. Their philosophy was, "My *uncle* will take care of me." The phrase meant "Uncle Sam," or the United States government, which sent them welfare checks. More kids meant a larger welfare check. Thankfully, I was too afraid to follow through with early offers to have sex. While having a child as a teenager and/or before marriage is not ideal, it is also not a death sentence. It requires more coordination to manage but it is indeed manageable.

I wouldn't change growing up in a single-family home with my dad. It gave me a wealth of perspective of the value that fathers bring to a family. He showed me firsthand how to treat people fairly, even if we had been mistreated. I never saw him treat my mom with anything but respect. He was adamant that we were to treat her with the utmost respect despite some of the decisions she made.

I could go on with other examples, but these are enough to show that many of my perceived shortcomings that challenged me in different ways during various phases of my life were also remarkably rewarding and have contributed to the character and attitude of the man I am today. The wealth of knowledge I gained from the experiences deepened my respect for other Hidden Gems. I was rich all along and didn't always know it!

Hidden Gems, recognize the many ways that you are already wealthy and use that to increase your confidence. You have something to offer the world, and that value needs to be exposed. Draw on the strengths that have gotten you through your life to this point, and don't diminish what you have accomplished to overcome some of your struggles.

Gem Seekers, realize that true wealth benefits others. Sharing what you have doesn't make you less rich. On the contrary, it increases your wealth and the wealth of those around you. Recognize and appreciate the wealth Hidden Gems can bring and help them build on their experience to continue to solve problems and take steps forward to get to the next levels. Genuine verbal support and encouragement goes a long way to build confidence.

☀ **Words of Wisdom** ☀
"Neither wealth nor poverty can be measured solely in financial terms."
-Ronnie Stallworth, Sr.

Think Big and Make It Happen

I have consistently stated that the success of Hidden Gems is linked to their exposure to higher-level thinking. That's certainly true, but there are other contributing factors. To a large degree, the success of Hidden Gems is dependent on their level of trust. Sometimes they can't envision themselves having the ability to achieve a super stretch goal. Hidden Gems must have an appetite for taking calculated risks versus clinging too tightly to a comfortable position. The simple statement to "think big" and make it happen can be terrifying.

This advice couldn't be more accurate than when I started working with the other managers, engineers, and scientists at the company headquarters in Des Plaines, Illinois. It didn't take long for me to realize my engineering degree wouldn't be enough for me to quickly advance through the ranks in the company. I had grown leaps and bounds while on the road and learned a ton from multiple unique and high-pressure situations. My interpersonal skills and my ability to resolve complex issues in a calming and collaborative manner prompted my managers to assign me to our most dissatisfied and challenging refinery and petrochemical clients. The high-pressure troubleshooting assignments routinely gave me an opportunity to hone my soft/essential skills and also deepen my technical knowledge. However, a key missing ingredient was understanding the underlying business principles behind many of the company's decisions. It wasn't necessarily that my peers were more business savvy than I was; we were all relatively equal. However, I was still a Hidden Gem. I had transitioned in from an outside office, and felt I needed to bring significantly more to the table to differentiate myself from others. I had a "working from behind" mentality as opposed to feeling content that being equal was good enough.

With that realization, I sat down with my family and talked through getting a master's degree, a mere four years after I had finally completed my bachelor's degree. With my family's support, I scheduled a meeting with my primary mentor, Norv Givens. He was a seasoned vice president for one of the divisions. We reviewed my career development plan for the next three to five years. It confirmed my assessment that I needed to improve my business acumen by getting a master's degree in business administration (MBA). However, what we didn't agree on was the school of choice. My stretch goal was to get into a top 50 business school to get my MBA, but he was adamant that I needed to target a top five business school. Even though I trusted his leadership, his recommendation immediately generated feelings of inadequacy. Irrespective of the success I had clearly realized, I still didn't feel like I belonged at a top five school or in some of the top business-level job roles. I constantly whispered to myself that others were smarter, better groomed, and overall, better suited than I was. This insecurity routinely resurfaced when I was faced with a significant professional challenge. I had zero confidence that I would get accepted to a top five business school, primarily because my undergraduate GPA was only 2.6. I was a logical thinker, so to me the probability of acceptance was essentially zero, but that was my limited perspective.

Norv didn't seem to care about my GPA. He had graduated from Northwestern University's Kellogg business school and suggested that I apply there as a starting point. Based on his recommendation, I initially considered Kellogg, Harvard Business School, the University of Chicago (Booth School of Business) and the University of Pennsylvania (Wharton). Any of these schools would provide an outstanding learning experience and propel my resume and credentials to a level that few others could reach. After doing some research, attending a few classes, and speaking with school staff and alumni, without a doubt the University of Chicago Booth School of Business was my first choice.

Even with the longshot of getting accepted, an equally daunting hurdle was overcoming the $126,000 cost for the program. The executive leadership team for my company, a wholly owned subsidiary of the parent company, sponsored two students each year to attend either Kellogg or Booth. However, the sponsorship program only targeted high-potential employees that had a proven track record. They were hand-picked by the executive leaders and there was a five-year backlog of candidates waiting for their turn to get their company sponsored MBA. After doing a bit more research, I found a tuition reimbursement program being offered by the parent company, but no one from my company had attempted to use the parent company's tuition assistance. Without asking for permission, I applied for the program and, to my surprise, qualified per the parent company guidelines.

I submitted my application to Booth along with three required essays. I ignored most of the recommended writing styles I had researched online and simply wrote from my heart with a focus on what I could bring to the class rather than what I would take away. I included information about my thinking style, my passion for helping others, and how my upbringing would be a significant benefit to my classmates. I also needed one personal and two professional letters of recommendation. Professionally, I received one from my mentor and one from the vice president of my department. Personally, I received a glowing letter of recommendation from former University of South Alabama president Gordon Moulton.

With the outstanding letters of recommendation from prominent Gem Seekers who unequivocally expressed their trust in my abilities, and my essays from the heart that articulated how my unusual background would bring value to the class, I was accepted into the University of Chicago Booth School of Business Executive MBA program in 2007. These sequences of events were more examples of Gem Seekers helping me reach heights that I never dreamed were possible!

From the moment I walked onto campus to start the MBA program, I was laser-focused with the full intent of completing it in the normal 21-month window. That was my promise to my family. The courses were intense, and the amount of rigor was equivalent to anything I had endured in engineering school. Booth was ranked #1 for a reason!

I was about halfway through the Executive MBA program when I was offered the expatriate assignment in Singapore that would allow my entire family to relocate to the capital of Kuala Lumpur in Malaysia. As a family, we discussed the opportunity to live abroad all together and quickly agreed that the boys would benefit from going to an international school, and Gina could focus on completing her master's since by law she couldn't work in Malaysia. The Booth staff was fantastic; they allowed me to switch from Chicago to the campus in Singapore at the midway point in 2008. I commuted from Kuala Lumpur to attend classes in Singapore one week out of every five. Changing campuses gave me another opportunity to work and interact in an Asian culture. Many aspects of academics and culture are different there than in the US, including logic and rationale when problem-solving, responding to questions more discreetly, showing greater respect for elders, and being more knowledgeable of international and geographic influences in the world.

As promised to my family, I graduated on time in March 2009 with my MBA. The entire experience was phenomenal! Getting an MBA from Chicago Booth has had as great an impact on my success as any other professional decision I made. There were three key unexpected lessons from the journey that helped me appreciate the experience even more.

First, preconceived thoughts can be crippling. I walked into the auditorium on the first day of classes and took a seat in a location that made me feel less vulnerable. I looked around the lecture hall and marveled at the diversity. The class makeup of the Chicago campus represented more than 50 different nationalities. As students introduced themselves and spoke about their successful careers, I was in awe of how many presidents, vice presidents, and general managers of Fortune 500 companies were represented. Others were highly successful physicians, hospital administrators, entrepreneurs, and attorneys. And then there I was, a simple manager and 2.6 GPA engineer. As the introductions propagated around the class and came closer to my turn to speak, my feelings of inadequacy caused me to heat up like a stove. I was sweating profusely, and my hands were shaking so much I couldn't even take a sip of water to help me settle down. I stumbled through my introduction, truncating it to get the spotlight off my lack of corporate stature and accomplishments. I couldn't do anything at that moment to convince myself I belonged among that group of established professionals.

When the professor announced our first break of the day, the sighs of relief could be heard from the other end of the building. We were all mentally exhausted from the initial couple of hours. It was intense! During the break, a dozen or so classmates gathered in one corner and openly questioned if they were worthy of being in the class. As it turned out, I wasn't the only one with an inferiority complex. Several students came over to introduce themselves and expressed their admiration of me being an engineer. "I could never do engineering. It's too hard and I hate math." "I feel so out of place," said one of the vice presidents of a major pharmacy. Another student said to me, "I read your bio in our cohort directory, and I can't believe how much you've accomplished in your life. I feel so privileged." Despite the mountain of data that confirmed my success, I had again found ways to devalue and marginalize my achievements. I did belong, just as much as the others, and it took my classmates to help me shake off my insecurities. Self-doubt is extremely difficult to overcome. Even when people constantly give positive encouragement, it can take years to eradicate.

Second, there are always going to be pseudo-leaders, success-blockers, and people who let jealousy get the best of them. Following one of our classes, I met some of my classmates at a nearby restaurant for dinner and drinks. Students from the current MBA cohort (my classmates) commonly met there to mingle with the earlier cohort that was one year ahead of us. As I was sitting with a few of my classmates, I noticed two familiar faces from my office approaching our table. Unbeknownst to me at the time, they were the two company-sponsored colleagues in the earlier cohort who were midway through the program. I could tell from the salty looks on their faces that they were perturbed to see me in the next batch of MBA students. The short list of exclusive, company-sponsored students was revered and, to some of the select few that received it, worn as a badge of honor. They knew I wasn't one of the "chosen" high-potential candidates. One of them was so infuriated that he crashed the conversation I was having with my classmates. He asked rapid-fire questions, demanding to know how I was able to get in the program when they had to wait for five long years on a waiting list. He was pissed.

Knowing they had only ill intentions, I was careful to keep my responses to a minimum. I barely knew them at work and they both routinely walked by me in the office hallways and never even uttered a simple hello. Realizing they weren't getting the answers they wanted, they switched tactics. One of them whispered to me that he would let me have his old exams, so I'd have an advantage in my class. It's common for some professors to reuse test questions from cohort to cohort. I declined his empty and manipulative offer loud enough for everyone at the table to hear. As they scurried away in frustration, my classmates laughed at their interrogation. They joked that jealousy and selfishness can make hand-chosen and high-performing future executives look like middle schoolers.

The third key takeaway from the program involved my confidence in sharing my knowledge. I learned an enormous amount of information that drastically improved my business acumen. At the same time, if I lacked the confidence to speak up and apply what I had learned, the impact of my hard work would be significantly diminished. I gained a tremendous amount of confidence through interactive collaboration with my classmates. They also had a strong appetite for continuous improvement, and it helped me develop the confidence to speak up and share my perspectives. My opinions added value and exposure irrespective of who I communicated with. Toward the end of the program, I began speaking up in meetings with executives at work in situations where I had previously never uttered a word before, and it was primarily driven by my increased confidence.

#getamentor, #bringmoretothetable, #mustkeepgrowing, #overcomeinadequacy, #workingfrombehind, #confidencematters

Leaders challenge the status quo, even in our thinking and expectations, to push beyond our comfort zone. My mentor, Norv Givens, could see far more potential in me than I had even considered. Not only did he believe I could get an MBA, but he also believed that I could hold my own in one of the top business schools in the nation, as did the former president of my undergraduate school. Because of their belief in me, it gave me more confidence to follow their lead. I was then able to expand and contribute my knowledge to help my company make good, sound decisions and positive changes that would go on to impact our customers and employees. Sometimes, we must trust leaders with our careers, even if we can't see where they are leading us at the time.

☀ **Words of Wisdom** ☀
"If we set our goals based solely on what we know today, without collaborating with others that have higher level thinking, we will consistently underachieve our capabilities."
-Ronnie Stallworth, Sr.

Live a Bucket-List Life

One of my favorite quotes is: "Happiness will never come to those who don't appreciate what they already have." Admittedly, I haven't always appreciated the blessings that I had. Certainly, more credit goes to my dad for helping shepherd me through my tough early years to set the foundation for my current life. Because of his influence, I've done my best to get the most out of life on a daily basis versus waiting for some seemingly perfect point in time, which rarely happens.

For myriad reasons, many Hidden Gems live their lives with a hustling and grinding mentality. Doing so is the trademark of some people growing up in poverty who have passion and energy to get more out of life but are slowed by inefficiencies.

A hustle-and-grind mentality is required to get through certain challenges in our journey. At the same time, our mentality must change over time for us to continue growing. The old adage of too much of anything can be bad also holds true for staying fixated on a certain type of lifestyle. A negative consequence of keeping your head down, grinding and hustling day in and day out without taking some time to enjoy the fruits of your labor, is waking up one day and realizing you've missed precious moments you can never get back.

Even in the toughest of times, we cannot go indefinite stretches without taking breaks to enjoy what a particular season of life has to offer. I hustled about as hard as anyone at certain points in my life, but I also took calculated and strategic breaks to live a little along the way, smell the roses, and explore new ways of thinking. Exposure brought perspective to what my life could be! The teenage version of myself was incapable of imagining the kind of life I've actually lived. I was underprivileged, shackled by illiteracy in my early childhood years, and my view of life was through a very narrow aperture. I didn't have the perspective to envision any version of myself becoming a chemical engineer, getting an MBA from one of the most prestigious business schools, and becoming vice president of a Fortune 100 company. I was not motivated to strive for something I didn't know existed. I didn't know what I didn't know, and it wasn't until later in life that I developed the mindset of "Think big and make it happen."

There is an aspect of my life that's even more important to me than living my bucket-list life—it's my family. Ronnie Jr. and Jonathan have been remarkably blessed as we've traveled the world, lived in million-dollar estate homes in gated communities, and physically touched almost all of the Seven Wonders of the World. Their perspectives as young adults are drastically different from anything I could have imagined at their age, and it has contributed to their motivations and successes.

Ronnie Jr. has a beautiful family and is a successful professional for a global IT firm. Although many of our characteristics are similar with regard to being humble, compassionate, and thoughtful of others, he is much more intelligent than I am. He is internally driven to be successful at whatever he touches. Ronnie and his family will live their best life, and I envision Ronnie being one of the most philanthropic givers of his generation.

Jonathan is remarkably creative, which is another credit to my ex-wife for this trait. Like Ronnie Jr., he is extremely intelligent, has a caring heart, and coupled with his creativity, will someday surpass any level of success and achievements that I've experienced. I am convinced that one of his creations will significantly change the world. His runway for future success is unbound!

Although my journey in life has been remarkably rewarding, there are not so subtle points of differentiation that are worth highlighting. Travel, exposure, and experiences are most meaningful when they are shared with family and friends. The top ten items on my bucket list are not solo activities. All of them have an outward-focused element that includes enabling, sharing, and/or experiencing them with someone else. For example, I loved visiting the Taj Mahal. However, it is still on my checklist of places to visit with my family. The experience wasn't the same because it was a missed opportunity to have my family experience the enormity and immaculate beauty of the structure and the friendly, welcoming Indian culture with me in the process.

Enjoying the journey is part of making the journey. While you want to keep your eye on the future, you also need to be aware of the present, in tune to know that every moment is an opportunity to learn and grow if you are paying attention. Tomorrow isn't promised, and some windows of opportunity are temporary. When they close, they close forever. It can be scary to say yes if you feel like you aren't ready, but sometimes you just have to take that leap of faith. Thank God I took advantage of opportunities along the way versus always waiting until the timing was perfect. We should live our daily lives with a sense of purpose!

※ **Words of Wisdom** ※
"If you truly want to know the culture,
you've got to live like the locals."
-Ronnie Stallworth, Sr.

EPILOGUE: WE CAN'T BOIL THE OCEAN

A number of years ago when I first started thinking about writing a book, my aperture was too broad. What started out as a modest writing project with a few simple objectives quickly morphed into a monumental effort. The energy required to write an entire book became so overwhelming that my scattered pages of notes and journaling sat dormant for nearly 18 years. I came up with one excuse after another to avoid tackling it until a close friend of mine introduced me to a writing coach, KishaLynn Elliott. After my initial meeting with KishaLynn, her first question to me was "Ron, what do you want readers to get from your *first* book?" She said it with a hint of sarcasm, but her message was loud and clear. I felt an immediate sense of relief. In the following days,

I went through a range of emotions all the way from joy about finally getting started in a meaningful way to being disappointed in myself for not being able to see the project in the context of smaller, more manageable parts. All I needed to do was focus on a few words at a time to make a sentence, string together a few sentences to make a paragraph, and in a matter of days, I would have had a chapter. As simple as it sounds now, I had done myself what I was advising others against—thinking about the big picture, the final product, in aggregate, instead focusing on smaller elements.

KishaLynn was a godsend! Based on her advice, I accepted the approach of using a second book to provide a detailed and very specific list of traits and attributes to more accurately identify Hidden Gems when they are in grade school and as young adults. And also, through my experiences, my next book will provide a similar list of very simple and easy-to-follow steps for people that want to become better Gem Seekers but don't know how to get started, don't have a lot of time to do volunteer work, and/or don't want to simply give away cash as a one-off band-aid approach. We can all benefit from positive constructive advice that's customized for a specific season of life. With KishaLynn's advice, I embarked on the 19-month journey of writing my first book, *Cracks in the Wall*, to highlight the impact that my dad had on my life, show how others helped me along the way, and stress the importance of incremental improvement. I used real-life examples, adventures, and a range of experiences to get points across in different ways. I showed the impact of others helping a poor, snotty-nosed kid from a poor neighborhood who most people thought would amount to nothing, instead ended up helping hundreds of others through scholarships, mentoring, and creating a foundation and other forms of philanthropy. Helping just one person made a positive difference in the lives of hundreds of other people.

My kids have always known me to help people when they have car trouble or are going through difficult financial times, or when people are struggling with issues and need someone to talk to. Over the years, I've changed dozens of tires, hopped out to help push stalled cars out of a busy intersection, and driven to a local store to purchase a gasoline can and fill it up with gasoline for a stranded motorist. I've let my kids call the highway department when we've seen large debris in the highway that could cause an accident. We've seen everything from mattresses to car bumpers in the middle of the expressway during heavy traffic. Rather than drive around it and forget it like most other motorists, I had my sons call it in. These are things I call my good deed for the day. I purposely let my sons see that there are plenty of things we can do to change the part of the world we live in. In many cases, the good deeds didn't require financial wealth, remarkable intelligence, or significant time commitment, but only a desire to do a good deed in a safe and easy manner.

I'm a firm believer that most people on this earth are good-hearted, want to help others, and want to earn their way. The following moments of disappointment, counterintuitive thinking, and random acts of kindness really exemplify the roller coaster ride of emotions that we face in our journey to become better people and when we attempt to help others. They are important because even when we are only attempting to change the small world we live in, we realize we cannot do everything. There will always be outliers that we must move on from.

In the first case, I had a conversation with Ray, a person I've been helping periodically for about 15 years. It's reflective of the types of conversations we can have that give us a reality check. Ray had gone through tough times in his adult life, including spending multiple stints in prison. He was recently released from prison and moved to my hometown. When he asked if I could help him out, it was a no-brainer. To my knowledge, Ray had always been respectful toward me and showed appreciation for what I had done, so I was happy to help him get a fresh start. I have several vacant lots that require monthly lawn maintenance. It takes about 15 minutes to run the lawn mower over each lot, with no requirements to bag grass clippings or leaves. It's straight-forward. Simply start the mower and, within 15 minutes, he would have earned $40. I also gave him permission to use my lawn mower and new weed trimmer to do other lawns in the area to earn additional cash. Things were working well, and I paid him for the four months that he cut the grass.

In another sign of good fortune, Ray landed a well-paying job (with the help of a family friend) using the skills he learned growing up working on cars to really show the value he could bring to the friend's business. As a result of Ray's good work, he was rewarded with a full-time job, plus another 20-25 hours a week overtime. The friend gave Ray the additional hours to help pay for his own apartment since he was temporarily staying with a family member. It was nearly the perfect scenario and the type of opportunity that can really catapult a Hidden Gem to another level of growth and development!

About three months after Ray had started his new job, I called him the same morning I was writing this epilogue of *Cracks in the Wall* to let him know that I'd be dropping by later in the day to pick up my lawn mower and weed trimmer for a few hours. A recent hurricane had left debris and toppled two trees on my vacant lots. Ray immediately said, "Ronnie, I don't have your stuff." Not quite understanding his response, I told him I had no issue driving over to grab them from the storage unit and he was free to continue using them when I was done. He quickly replied, "No, you are not hearing what I said. I pawned them and also your chain saw that you had in the storage unit. I had lost my job and was running low on cash, so I took them to the pawn shop." Trying to make sense of the situation, I calmly asked if he had ever asked me for money or anything else that I didn't give him without questioning what it was for. He replied "No, you've always given me money and helped me." It was a simple conversation yet with logic I could not understand. He ought to have known I would help him if he asked, as I had done before, but instead he chose to pawn my items for cash, something he had no right to do.

There are a lot of people, including me, that suffer, struggle, and go through tough times, but we realize taking something that doesn't belong to us is wrong. And doing it to someone that is going out of their way to help only makes the act more reprehensible. Ray said, "I'm sorry, but I had no choice but to pawn them. I was in a tough situation." His complete lack of awareness for what he had done, and the absence of any remorse were appalling. If he had said he made a mistake, would get another job and replace the items, I would have been about 90% in his corner. The real issue is that Ray does not know when he is doing wrong, and that is a major problem. There is a huge difference between Ray and Tina in the chapter *Don't Let Perfect Get in the Way of Getting Better*. A good rule of thumb is, you have a better chance of helping someone who knows the difference between right and wrong (even if they occasionally do wrong) versus a person that is oblivious to screwing someone over, because the latter is analogous to driving on a busy highway with no lane markers, guard rails, or rumble strips to tell them when they are running off the road. Sometimes we must accept defeat and look for someone else to help.

The next example I want to highlight is one of my church members at Willow Creek Community Church in South

Barrington, Illinois. His name is Al, and he is over 90 years old. After serving as a greeter in the morning, Al moves over to the cafeteria and voluntarily picks up trays when people are finished eating. He takes the empty trays over to the disposal station. It's a self-service cafeteria and churchgoers are expected to take their own trays to the disposal area when they are done. Nevertheless, Al volunteers to take care of the trays for dozens of visitors each Sunday. In Al's mind, he is simply taking advantage of his free time between the services to do a good deed. His efforts rarely go unnoticed. Also, Al routinely invites churchgoers to his retirement village for lunch. I have gone several times and he always uses his monthly stipend to cover the tab. What Al is doing is changing *his* world. I won't ever forget the hospitality he showed me and the hundreds of lives he has touched over the years, including giving guided tours of his home at Friendship Village to prospective residents. Al is a living example of changing the world!

The third example I want to mention occurred following the 2016 presidential election. A business school alum made the statement that he was so frustrated with the outcome of the election that he was not going to do anything for the next four years. He felt overwhelmed that a Republican had won, so he made a declaration to sit idle until the 2020 election. He was only going to support a Democrat as President of the United States. I asked him what he had done during the previous eight years when we had a Democrat as President of the United States. The real answer was essentially nothing. In reality, some people will use any reason to do nothing. There was absolutely nothing blocking him from doing good deeds in his local community, church group, circle of local friends, or even volunteering at a food pantry. I heard Republicans say the same thing in 2012 when their candidate lost. In other words, irrespective of who is in the White House, there are literally hundreds of smaller positive and meaningful actions we can take to continue making incremental progress as humans caring for our world and its inhabitants.

My fourth example relates to me directly. When I was at the University of South Alabama, I wanted to make a difference by giving back to the university. A number of affluent donors contributed millions of dollars to fundraising campaigns. I wanted to do the same but certainly didn't have millions of dollars to donate. I started with a $500 chemical engineering scholarship. It was really to change the world for a small group of students like me that had some financial difficulties but were working and weren't likely to qualify for any academic scholarships. Like me, they had to work for a living, had families, and had more modest GPA's. This small initial investment quickly morphed into a full endowment thanks to Charlie Kipling, a very generous donor who learned about the challenges I had gone through to complete my engineering degree. Not only did Mr. Kipling change the world I live in, but he also changed the world for dozens of Hidden Gems who have received the Ron Stallworth Chemical Engineering scholarship since 2004. Mr. Kipling is changing the world!

My final example occurred during severe flooding in the Houston, Texas, area several years ago. A close friend of mine, Slade Hall, decided to tow his boat from his home in Baton Rouge to help rescue victims stranded in the flood. No one asked him to do it. Slade is a good-hearted person, and people were in need of help quickly, so he immediately jumped into action to help. Timing was critical and there were no direct orders from the President of the United States, the Texas governor, or local officials regarding travel from nearby areas. Considering the severity of the situation, Slade changed his world and the world of dozens of others in the Houston area by his purposeful acts of kindness. Slade is changing the world!

I give my thanks to God, my dad, and the many other Gem Seekers that have helped me along the way. I've gone from being a Hidden Gem, not knowing my own potential and struggling to overcome immense odds, to becoming a Gem Seeker that is determined to help improve the world for thousands of others. With this book I am expanding my platform to help inspire more Gem Seekers to take one more step, and to inspire Hidden Gems to show a little more of who you are by reaching out to a person you see as a mentor. None of these things are earth-shattering. However, they are helping improve the world we live in. At a minimum, they are helping us appreciate the great lives we have. We really can do something to save the world. To the Gem Seekers and Hidden Gems throughout this book, people serving in the military, educators, law enforcement personnel, healthcare workers, scientists, entrepreneurs, philanthropists, volunteers, and countless others who go out of the way to help others, thank you for finding the cracks in the walls we encounter and breaching them to make our world a better place!

☀ **Words of Wisdom** ☀
"Rarely do we achieve anything of significant success without the help of others."
-Ronnie Stallworth, Sr.

THE END.

ABOUT THE AUTHOR

Ronnie "Ron" Stallworth, Sr. and his three older brothers were raised in poverty by an elderly single father. Despite obstacles that included racism, illiteracy, and homelessness, Ron's Dad taught him lessons that would bolster him through these challenges and propel him to achieve an education and become a successful engineer and vice president of a Fortune 100 company. Ron earned his Bachelor of Science in chemical engineering from the University of South Alabama, and an MBA from the University of Chicago Booth School of Business. Ron has lived and/or worked in over 70 countries. A Hidden Gem turned Gem Seeker, he established the Ron Stallworth Chemical Engineering Scholarship endowment at the University of South Alabama in 2005. Ron has two sons and a daughter who is deceased. He still lives in Mobile, Alabama. *Cracks in The Wall* is his first published book.

Made in the USA
Middletown, DE
12 September 2021